Want a Job?
Get Some Experience.
Want Experience?
Get a Job.

Want a Job?
Get Some Experience.
Want Experience?
Get a Job.

Don Berliner

amacom

**A Division of
American Management Associations**

to didi

Library of Congress Cataloging in Publication Data

Berliner, Don.
    Want a job? Get some experience. Want experience?
Get a job.

    Includes index.
    1. Applications for positions. 2. Employment inter-
viewing. I. Title.
HF5383.B425   650'.14   78-18304
ISBN 0-8144-5474-7

Second Printing

Acknowledgments

THERE are some people who deserve special thanks for having helped bring this book to fruition.

Diane, my wife, endured through all my job-hunting and book-writing adventures, giving me an abundant supply of love and support. In sharing my disappointments and frustrations, as well as my fun and success, she never lost faith in me and was always ready to offer constructive criticism. I can't thank her enough.

Harry and Gladys Berliner, my folks, who must have been initially shocked at the idea of their sonny boy becoming unemployed for a while, were the kind of parents who tried to nurture whatever awakening interests I developed as I grew up. Helen and Lou Snyder, Diane's parents, also supported me enthusiastically. I don't think they quite anticipated what their daughter was getting herself into with me.

Larry Weiner, my very good friend of many years, who shared many of my adventures along the rocky job-hunting road, provided some useful ideas and was often a good sounding board.

The others in my family, both blood and in-law, and my other very good friends deserve my thanks for their constant interest in and enthusiasm for what I was doing.

John Lee, a financial editor at *The New York Times,* devoted valuable time and effort in showing a greenhorn freelance something about writing.

Miriam Klipper, a former editor at a New York publishing house, showed enthusiastic interest in my original idea and persuaded the greenhorn to write up a detailed chapter outline. Though her publishing house didn't buy the book, Miriam's help was invaluable in getting me to push ahead. Steve Ross, editor of *New Engineer,* made some very helpful suggestions, one of which led me to AMACOM's door.

Eric Valentine, my editor at AMACOM, with wit, judgment, and helpful guidance coordinated the entire project. It was sometimes tiring, but always a pleasure, to work with Eric.

Judy Cuddihy spent many hours helping to reorganize the material. Her clear thinking and sense of humor contributed a lot to the final manuscript.

Ria Trinkle, my typist, stayed with me through several drafts and performed admirably under tight deadlines.

And, finally, I must take this opportunity to humbly thank all of the many people I encountered throughout my own job-hunting efforts. I certainly owe thanks to all the company interviewers, personnel people, agency middlemen, and somber book and article writers who, though unintentionally, provided the basis for much of the material. Without them, this book would surely not have been written.

Don Berliner

Contents

1 / Introduction

THE title of this book was inspired by the frustrated musings of a friend of mine who, finding himself laid off after a short taste of his first "real" job, was struck by the vicious circularity of many job-hunting situations. It would be amusing if it weren't so true; employment markets are loaded with catch-22's that can trap the brand-new and even the experienced job hunter. Job hunting and people hiring are games played chiefly by humans, not computers. As a result, human nature—capricious, fickle, and emotional as it can be—often creeps into the process. But this doesn't mean a job hunter has to like it or to stand idly by, shaped and bent by the whole process without knowing what is going on.

While the idea for this book was turning around in my mind, I too was looking for a job. It's no accident, then, that most of the book was prompted by my own experiences. I didn't know how typical they were until, in talking with others who were either voluntarily or involuntarily in the same boat, I was assured that many of the incidents were shared and common. Ordinarily such camaraderie would be comforting. And it was, but more important, it was illuminating. I think it is easy to miss or forget some of the lessons of job hunting. Sometimes, these lessons can be useful, though often the best that can be salvaged is a laugh or two.

I don't claim to have become an expert at all—it's just that I've picked up some information along the job-hunting trail that may be helpful to others. I only hope to point out some of the pitfalls and pratfalls along the way and how you can avoid them.

A word to those people presently or potentially involved in the job-hunting game from the other side of the desk—yes, I mean those doing the hiring. (Even though you may be looking for a job today, you could be the one looking for the candidate tomorrow.) Maybe I would not have been so impelled to write this book if there were very few shenanigans going on in the job market. However, since these things are occurring in some form or another (perhaps not precisely as depicted in this book), I hope that even those playing the game from the hiring side can see the humor (and irony) in much of it. Actually, it should be easier for someone who is not out hustling and rustling in the job-hunt pits. Anyway, it would sure be nice if they, too, could indulge in some introspective giggles.

And, as a final thought, if these people, recognizing the problems that exist, would think twice before adding to them or creating new ones, the entire game could become more of an earnest but good-natured exchange of information for both sides.

All right, let's get down to business. The book is organized in a logical procession of subject areas—writing a resume, cultivating references, digging up leads, dealing with middlemen, getting the interviews, going for interviews, handling and interpreting interviews, getting the job offers, and (ah, yes!), accepting the offer, negotiating the terms, and finally showing up Monday morning to begin the new job. There's a lot to do, so let's get started!

2 / Resumes and References

YOUR resume is an almost inescapable element of job hunting; it's not exactly your key to success, but it will often help you get beyond the front door. It is an advertisement of yourself, describing your personal qualifications and professional abilities to your audience of potential employers. It is read by a company representative who decides whether or not he will call you for an interview.

Obviously, a resume is important; however, you should not stand in awe of it. Used properly, it can make your job hunt much easier. Remember, there are many effective ways to organize your resume to make it work to your advantage. The particular style and content you use depends on you.

Begin with Personal Information

Of course your name and address will appear at the beginning of the resume. But do you really need to title it "Resume" or "Work History" or "Employment Experience"? Forget it—you can rest assured that the company person will be able to recognize a resume without being told.

What other personal items do you need to include? Phone number, height, weight, birth date, citizenship, marital status, social security number, age, annual income . . . wait a minute, this isn't an application for a dating service (although there are certain similarities). Let's leave a little mystery; if you reveal everything, there will be fewer personal questions an interviewer can ask you later. Pick a few personal items and put them in. It is a way of personalizing your resume and gives the reader a sense that he is finding out about a real live person.

You may have noticed that the list of items includes both birth date *and* age. Superfluous? Certainly not! As communications experts and college lecturers alike have long noticed, in order to communicate certain information, it is often necessary to repeat the same facts two or three times and in two or three different ways. Many times, I've had an interviewer ask my age after having just scanned a resume containing my birth date. Either he didn't trust his arithmetic ability or he was merely testing my memory and consistency.

I think it is safe to say, though, that you don't need to include very personal items like the location of significant birthmarks, the number of children by a previous marriage, or a list of medications you have taken within the past six months. You can omit such information from your resume without harming your chances. And don't attach a snapshot of yourself either. There is really nothing to be gained by it. Besides, do you want to be thought of as just a pretty face?

After revealing these personal tidbits, you should consider including a capsule summary of your career goals and professional aspirations. For some people, it can be an important way of establishing a focus in your resume. This is where you can express your ideal career future, in contrast, perhaps, to your less than ideal past. Here you are the defense lawyer making a summation before the jury. The opposition cannot object because the admissibility of facts is not a question at this point. In your resume you have the advantage of placing your "summation" near the beginning of your argument so as to influence the jury early on—before you present the facts. This will help them interpret the evidence that you will be presenting later.

There's a lot of leeway in describing your ideal career. You can give a broad generalization of the position you would like—for instance, "Work in a profit-oriented organization in such a capacity as to use a graduate business education in a position offering early responsibility and wide exposure in a corporate planning environment." Perhaps you prefer a hard-and-fast, down-to-earth description: "Employment as an executive trainee in sales planning for a Northeast non-industrial-oriented, diversified Fortune 100, packaged goods, multinational, vertically integrated organization." (Whew!)

You could also describe more than one position in hopes that one of them will hit the mark. But this is tricky, because you don't want a list that's too varied or too lengthy. An employer who sees jack-of-all-trades on your resume may consider you just plain wishy-washy. (If you are shooting for more than one type of job, just make up two or three different resumes, each with its own career objective.) The point is, when describing your career goal, include those things that can't easily be summarized elsewhere. If your resume is thorough enough, skip the career goal altogether.

The Resume Body—Give It Punch

Next comes the body of the resume, and at this point a well-known dilemma arises. Which should you present first, your education history or your job history? Of course, this assumes that you are far enough along in life to have this problem. A brand-new college graduate with no job history to speak of doesn't have a choice.

Usually the solution comes down to the question of which of the two is more impressive looking, in terms of sheer length, the impact of a particular name, or a more pleasing continuity of dates. But then what do you do if, for example, your work experience is longer than your schooling, but one of the schools you attended has a most prestigious sound to it? (We should all have this complication.) Or, more problematically, suppose your job history is longer than your educational history, but, at the same time, your job history is a bit erratic and shot with blanks here and there. The solution is simple if you remember that you are aiming mostly at the "hasty glancer" breed of resume reader. This is the person who loves (or, in all fairness, may be forced because of lack of time) to skim all the resumes that come along. Let's face it; the person who doesn't speed-read those re-

sumes will discover all the goods and not-so-goods
sooner or later. But it is the hasty glancer who must
glean from your resume the high and low points. So
what you should do is make it easy. Take advantage of
the skimmer's reading habits—accentuate the positives and, let us say, blend in the negatives so that at
the very least they don't stand out and catch the
reader's eye.

How does the skimmer's method affect the examples mentioned above? First of all, since the hasty
glancer is pressed for time, format may have more
effect than content. Thus the following are usually
considered the order of importance: length, name
impact, and continuity. In both of the previous
examples, I would still put the employment history
first because it is longer. The prestigious school will
stand out anyway. And the erratic nature of the
employment history will not be apparent to most
hasty glancers.

Incidentally, to help fill in some of the calendar
holes it is a good idea to indicate employment by years
rather than month-to-month. That is, write:

    1971–1972   Job X
    1968–1970   Job Y

rather than:

    November 1971–February 1972   Job X
    August 1968–February 1970   Job Y

Older applicants, who find their job-hunting efforts
bumping up against their age, might do well to omit
entirely any mention of jobs going back more than 15
or 20 years. You don't want to go out of your way to
broadcast your age, and this amount of time is certainly enough to suggest experience and maturity.

Besides, whittling down your experience keeps your resume to a manageable length. For the same reasons, why even mention the dates you graduated from school? Length can work to your disadvantage, so remember that potency counts more than completeness. Long paragraphs may make you appear terrific, but not if they go unread. And while we're talking about length, should you think about cutting your resume down before you start running on to a second page? Many authors of job-hunting manuals take great pains to warn against using a second page. I think they overdo it a bit. It is sometimes impossible to squeeze everything into a single page without it seeming very crowded. (Using a typewriter with a smaller type size can help, though it also decreases readability.) I don't worry too much if a resume requires that second page. I figure the thorough reader will absorb everything anyway. As for the glancer, how much longer does it take to skim an extra half page?

Along with the question of brevity comes that of detail. How much is really necessary or even desirable? If you find you can't explain an item easily, perhaps it is better not to try. Sometimes describing past deeds on paper is like explaining a good joke, which E. B. White likened to the delicate procedure of dissecting a frog—in the process you kill it. Don't overdo the detail; you'll want to explain things later in a personal interview anyway. Besides, why run the risk of insulting the intelligence of your resume reader by babying him with an overly detailed description of a job that presumably falls within his own field? Just sketch the basics.

Above all, don't present your job history as a simple laundry list of broad job duties. It is difficult for the resume reader to get excited over such dry descriptions. Light up that resume with *deeds,* not duties. Tell them what you did, not what you were supposed to do. Make liberal use of decisive, action-packed language to describe your accomplishments. Get across that you can develop, initiate, investigate, organize, analyze, supervise, direct, conceive, present, implement, change, design, create, plan, reduce (costs) and increase (profits)! Let your accomplishments and adrenaline spurt right off the page. Observe the difference between these two job descriptions:

> Assistant product manager for adult game manufacturer. Responsible for the games market oriented toward the 21 to 30 age group. Duties included the coordination of advertising, including approval of artwork and layout; communication with creators of new game ideas; and promotion planning for new products.

> As assistant product manager responsible for adult games aimed at 21- to 30-year-olds, supervised a $1.5 million advertising budget, from selection of artwork and layout to choice of appropriate media. Increased our share of market segment from 10% to 14% in 9 months. Directed development of two new game ideas from original conceptualization to finished product. Introduced a "Beat the Expert" promotion in 1,200 book and department stores nationwide, which received a 4-page spotlight write-up in *Game Play* magazine.

There's just more punch in the second description, because the accomplishments are tangible.

Reorganize Yourself—
The Accomplishment Resume

The resume format most familiar to resume writers and readers alike is the chronological one in which each past job is described separately and in reverse chronological order. However, there is a new trend today. No longer do you need to list your "Employment Experience." Now, you can describe your "Significant Areas of Accomplishment" or "Past Personal Achievements." Instead of segmenting your background job by job, show yourself as a *total person* by highlighting aspects of each job that relate to a particular skill. What am I talking about? Let me demonstrate.

Suppose your employment history is light—you have been a counselor at a summer camp, worked for a year as a hospital volunteer, engaged in various part-time endeavors. You glance through the traditional resume samples and discover how simple it is to compose an impressive one—provided you have at least six years' experience in a large corporation. Well, if you don't have this experience (or even if you have), why not use the "concept" approach? It goes like this:

AREAS OF ACCOMPLISHMENT

Communication Skills. Conducted in-patient admission interviews on a continuing basis to elicit medical history specifics. Also assisted nurses on floor duty.

Community Relations. Gained community understanding and experience through volunteer work at a busy downtown Chicago hospital.

Leadership and Cooperation. Developed cooperative skills in four-year association with Boy Scouts. Gained leadership experience as student council assistant secretary in high school.

Sales. Worked in hospital gift store and summer camp canteen concession. Monthly sales doubled during my tenure at the concession.

Management. Responsible for organization of patients' daily activities at medical institution. Patient participation increased 30 percent.

Public Relations. Learned how to handle people in face-to-face situations at city hospital and summer camp.

Office Skills. Persisted as assistant administrator at medical facility and summer camp and was a library aide at high school. Office machines used: electric typewriter, mimeograph, PA system.

Get the idea? Underline those individual skills and break down every job (or high school duty) you've ever had into its components. In the above example you have two jobs versus a half dozen or so emphasized skills. Also, someone seeing the *Leadership and Cooperation* category under AREAS of ACCOMPLISHMENT is bound to be more impressed than if he spotted a *Camp Minitoga* under EMPLOYMENT EXPERIENCE.

Be sure to take note of the length of the explanations in the example—short and sweet. You don't want to go into a song and dance routine in each paragraph. Besides requiring lengthy reading, this forces the reader to hunt for your attributes. The reasons he should hire you must be immediately apparent and compelling.

The accomplishment resume also allows you to soften the impact of certain embarrassing parts of your job history. Now it is no longer necessary to call attention to some unfortunate lapse of time occurring between jobs or, for that matter, a short period of time at one job. Instead, you can emphasize your performance on the job. This type of resume is particularly suitable for the individual who has been bouncing a bit from field to field and still wants to retain some semblance of order in his background. With an accomplishment resume you can accentuate those concepts around which you have built your career and oriented your life.

After the employment history hurdle—whether you opt for a chronological or a concept-oriented approach—many books would advise listing some personal interests, hobbies, and extracurricular activities. But how important is it if you played badminton in college or sang in the glee club? How relevant is your collection of Hungarian postage stamps?

Of course, this depends partly on the job you are applying for. If you had a habit of learning a different language every year, that would certainly be a reasonable asset. However, assuming you have the usual assortment of ordinary interests and activities, it doesn't make sense to present a long list of them. Space is valuable and you might just as well reserve it for other uses. Just throw in a couple of these items to make your resume appear more personal.

Naturally, if you can find something with which your potential interviewer could personally identify, that would be great. For example, a friend of mine is a member of a nationally chartered fraternity and is careful to include said fraternity on his resume. Without knowing for sure, he has a strong feeling that his resume is getting just a bit more attention as a result.

If you can dig up any inside information at all—from a present or former employee, a newspaper story, a company supplier—that pinpoints a particular interest, activity, or affiliation of the prospective reader of your resume, it may benefit you to slant it in that direction. But this can be a dangerous business; you can't be sure of just who in the company will see the resume and take part in the hiring decision. Several people may have conflicting allegiances.

Special Purpose Resumes and Some Oddball Advice

You may have heard of the "special purpose" resumes that have been touted by various resume-writing books or services. How about a resume that resembles a magazine (complete with table of contents and illustrations) or a news article (with headline, subhead, and the appropriate complimentary story)? Or a scrapbook resume, consisting of a dozen or so informative pictures of the applicant with appropriate captions; a resume that moves (it's on film); one that speaks (a tape recording); or one that moves *and* speaks (video tape)?

People are applying their imagination to the art of resume preparation in increasingly fanciful ways these days. I have heard some of the old-timers in the field reminisce about the unorthodox resumes they remember that, today, would hardly catch an eye.

One guy could still recall the ruckus made over a resume printed on pastel blue paper and another that came in on personable 6″ × 9″ paper instead of stodgy 8½″ × 11″. Actually, most companies seem to frown as much on these only slightly offbeat resumes as they do on the really exotic varieties.

But there are plenty of resume-writing services that attempt to push you into using one of the oddballs for the simple reason that, being different, you will stand out. True enough, but different doesn't mean unique. And uniqueness is what a company is looking for. Your resume will no doubt be noticed ("George, take a look at this—a resume shaped like a geodesic dome! I wonder how he got it into that manila envelope?"). It may even be saved as a curiosity. Yet, most companies are aware that creative packaging is very often used to sell a so-so product. So I would avoid the fancy resume package, unless you are applying to an advertising agency; they in particular may appreciate such nifty creativity.

I suppose the resume-writing services can be of assistance in some situations. Certainly, if you can get samples of some of the resumes they have created, you may be able to lift some of their concepts and adapt them to your own situation. Even some of their own promotional literature can help; it may prod you into better organizing your thoughts about yourself. Several services I know of provide a detailed questionnaire. Once you sign up, they use your answers to construct their version of your resume. As it turns out, the questionnaire itself can be instructive in getting you to think about yourself.

While we're on the subject of special purpose resumes, there is one problem they can help you solve.

Most of the things I have been concentrating on have been directed at the person who has an average, or less than average, amount of experience. But there is a chance (I can hear the laughter already) that some of you have encountered the problem of being *over-qualified*. Sometimes too much experience can produce a dangerous overload in the employer's circuitry. "What should I do?" you cry out. "It sounds like I have to have a dozen different resumes aimed at a dozen different companies!" That's the ticket! Take a hint from the fashion industry. There were the mini, midi, and maxi skirt lengths, each one revealing succeedingly less detail about the individual. Those with a mature enough resume body should consider using several different resumes. Where your experience seems light for the job, parade your mini before them and knock them out by revealing the most you can. Should you want to hide some things, display a discreet maxi and retain that element of the unknown. For a company you know nothing about, go middle-of-the-road. And be aware of any new style (resume, that is) that might give you an even better appearance.

Neatness Counts

Of course, in preparing your resume, you should avoid sloppiness and stinginess. Whoever types the resume should go nice and slow because mistakes will certainly be picked up by a company's fine tooth comb. Make sure those paragraph indentations are consistent (not five spaces here and six spaces there). Above all, don't just modify an old resume.

Yes, they can tell that, in a foolishly lazy mood, you created a new resume out of an old one by cutting it up into pieces and pasting it together again in a more coherent version (either the segmentation shows or the paste lumps up). Yes, they have seen the resume that is merely last year's version with an addendum typed at the end of it (either the added piece messes up the chronology of "last job first" or the type style and spacing of the addendum do not match the basic resume). And yes, they know all about the resume that was originally slanted toward another job and on which you have had to do a lot of underlining in order to attract your reader's eye to those parts relevant to the current situation (the irrelevancy of much of the material will be readily apparent). Resume alterations are quite obvious; I'd skip the tailoring and, instead, put together a new one entirely.

The Reference Bugaboo—Some Do's and Don'ts

"Listen, Sid," I inquire nervously, "do you mind if I use your name as a reference?"

Sid mutters, "Uh . . . yeah, I guess so; but I'm not sure we know each other well enough in a professional sense."

At this point, my palms sweaty, I wonder why Sid doesn't seem all that anxious to be a reference for me. Could it be that five years of working pratically side by side failed to create a professional bond that was strong enough? Maybe Sid doesn't express himself too well and doesn't feel he could do justice to my qualifications? Perhaps he is suspicious of reference checks altogether and, merely on principle, resents the bureaucracy for checking up on any of its citizens?

Well, as it turned out (I discovered through a third person), none of these reasons was correct. Sometimes the obvious is overlooked. Sid bore a long-standing grudge against me because of some unfortunate event four years ago and hadn't the guts to tell me so. As a reference, Sid would have had enormous credibility due to our five-year association—and he could have absolutely murdered my job hopes.

"Is there anyone we could contact who is familiar with you and has some knowledge of your past accomplishments?" This is the way the reference question is usually phrased. It helps to be prepared for this; it can hit you at any time. Some companies ask for references right off; others wait until you have been selected as the final candidate. The difference is that one company puts great stock in a recommendation, whereas the other goes through the motions as a virtual formality.

Also confusing are the types of references a company may desire. Each firm has varying opinions about what kind of person can or cannot be counted on to give the sort of reference the company thinks is meaningful. Thus some companies may discount completely any former or present employers, co-workers, relatives, close friends, neighbors, or landlords as references.

One firm that kept me chuckling had ruled out *all* of these categories. I carefully considered every possible reference I could think of, but every single one fell into one of those damned categories. How could they not? I finally recalled the name of a person I was not related to, no longer associated with closely, never worked for, worked with, lived near, or paid rent to. He was an old high school chum whom I hadn't seen in ten years. The experience gave me some insight into why a company would make such restrictions. Obviously this company was making use of the notions that: (1) any person whom you volunteer as a reference and who knows you well at all will give a biased, glowing report of your character; (2) a person's patterns and attitudes are well established early in life. Therefore the company would rather reap the best of both worlds by contacting someone who no longer knows you well but once did. The logic is appealing.

But once you do think of a suitable reference, how do you know he is going to speak highly of you, or, as they say, "give you good refs"? As the episode with Sid demonstrates, this is an important and sometimes difficult problem requiring you to somehow assess your reference's real opinion of you.

Suppose, for example, you discover that one of your references can only give a lukewarm recommendation. On the surface, this may not appear to be much of a problem. It's better, you think, than an ice-cold reference from someone who utterly despises you. Well, just barely. Of course it would be preferable to avoid a reference who is going to dramatically knife you in the back. But looking on the bright side, a completely negative reference can indicate positive things also. First, it shows that you weren't a quiet nobody, that you weren't a mental weakling, that you do possess a vibrant personality and occasionally stepped on a few toes. And secondly, it demonstrates moral courage and open-mindedness to select a reference who you knew might not have agreed with you on every company matter. A lukewarm reference, though, does not have the same implications as the ice-cold reference. Everything about it is subtle and hidden because of what remains unsaid. There is a lack of any excitement, negative or positive; there is neither enthusiastic affirmation nor bombastic criticism. The lukewarm reference is like a slow-acting poison. Therefore, when you go out to round up some references and you come across someone who hesitates just the slightest bit, pass him up and heave a thankful sigh of relief. Seek out the ref who, out of respect and admiration for you, is effectively enthusiastic. That's what you want spilling over to your potential employers.

How can you really determine your references' opinions of you? Presumably, in the first place, you won't use too many people you are not close to or sure of. As for the one or two uncertain ones, you might just call them up and ask. As a last resort, you could have a friend do it, preferably a friend who handles himself well on the telephone. The friend calls up in the guise of a potential employer doing a reference check on you. It is tricky and must be done very cautiously. The one and only time I did it for a friend, it went something like this:

"Mr. Holbrook, please."
"Yes, this is Mr. Holbrook. May I help you?"
"Mr. Holbrook, a Mr. Brown has applied to us for a job and he gave your name as a reference. I believe you are a former employer of his."
"Yes, that's correct. Sam was a pretty good worker. I

guess you would say he was the kind of guy who . . . by the way, to whom am I speaking?"

"Oh"—a nervous cough and a quick recovery—"I am Mr. Berliner of . . . of United Bushing. I work in the personnel department here and we're just doing a routine reference check on Mr. Brown."

"I see. Listen, could you hang on a moment, please?" After some paper shuffling, Mr. Holbrook is back.

"Mr. Berliner, I am very glad you called. There isn't enough I could say about Sam that would do justice to his qualifications—his diligence, intelligence, creativity, and above all, his sincerity and trustworthiness. He also has a warm sense of humor and can appreciate a good joke. Do you want me to continue? I really could go on at great length about Sam."

"No, that won't be necessary. As I mentioned, this is merely a routine check to ensure that there is nothing negative in Mr. Brown's background. Thank you very much for your time, Mr. Holbrook."

"That's quite all right. Anything I can do for Sam is my pleasure, believe me. Good-bye."

I hung up, confident that Sam's job offers would soon be rolling in. This guy seemed so positive about Sam. How could his attitude fail to come across to any prospective employer?

The trouble is, things are not always what they seem. It seems that soon Sam began having more trouble than before in getting job interviews, let alone job offers. Mysterious? Well, it turns out that the papers Holbrook was shuffling during our conversation happened to include a copy of Sam's resume. And on it, Sam the Brainless had inscribed the names of his references—a former co-worker, Mr. Holbrook, and *me!* After hearing my name, Holbrook found it on the resume and put two and two together. Annoyed at the situation, he bounced back by subtly humoring me, but to every other legitimate reference checker, he gave a devastating picture of Sam. Worst of all, he was smart enough not to lash out at Sam in a directly negative way. Instead, Holbrook extracted his revenge by relentlessly using the subtly-worded, lukewarm reference—what should really be called the luke-cold reference. Sam never had a chance.

The luke-cold reference points out one good reason for leaving references off your resume entirely. Another reason is the possibility that your references will change from time to time. (Sam's certainly did.) Anyway, I think it is preferable not to flaunt your references' names on a resume. If you feel you must cover yourself, indicate that "suitable references will be provided upon request" somewhere on your resume. An exception to this might be if you recently saved the life of the son of the AT&T chairman, and he insists you use him as a reference. Go ahead. Give him top billing in your resume. You saved his son's life. The least you can do is allow him to pay his debt of gratitude.

Some of you may be thinking that the whole idea of references is dubious anyway, that they are basically useless in judging someone's appropriateness for a job. Surely no one would supply the name of a reference who couldn't represent the applicant in a most glowing light. And except for a hermit, doesn't everyone have a few people to count on to volunteer superpositive recommendations? At first glance this seems self-evident.

But you are not giving your prospective company enough credit. I've often gotten caught in that trap myself. During one particular job-hunting period in

my life, I was in the fortunate position of having a
very solid set of references who were ready to vouch
most enthusiastically for the angelical nature of my
character and my strong business sense besides. Two
or three job interviews seemed to strike a positive note
between the interviewers and me. References were
asked for, and the names delightfully volunteered.
The jobs were of the broad, functional sort that require a generalist. From the job descriptions and the
tone of the interviews, I surmised that these companies and these particular interviewers were putting
a great deal of emphasis on the nature of the personality of the person they would eventually hire. It was
important that this person be professionally aggressive but personable and able to deal with people at all
levels. As a result, references would be an important
factor in the final selection.

With the kind of references I had, I knew there
was nothing to worry about. However, I had forgotten one fact that many job hunters lose sight of. Once
an interviewer has started looking into your
background, if he is smart, he will refuse to be led
around like a dog on a leash. It makes sense that a
company will be diligent in its efforts to unearth as
much information about you—good and bad—as it
can. And no matter how good your references are,
they can kill you if you are not supercareful.

For example, think about this variation. All a
clever personnel man has to do while talking to one of
your references is to ask whether there is anyone else
he can think of who might happen to know you, the
job hunter. Thinking that this request fits in with the
tone of the questioning, your reference cheerfully
complies (relieved that he hasn't let you down by

flunking this question) and volunteers a name or two. One of the names my super-supporter happened to pick was someone who indeed knew me but, alas, was not too thrilled with me. The rest of the story is obvious. I was tripped up by one of my reference's references—I was a victim of the *reference ricochet.*

So give a thought to those references. Who else do they know who knows you too? In this age of instant communication it is fantastically easy to bounce from a first-level reference to a second or even third level in the eternal search for truth.

Actually, this brings up another important point. If the reference ricochet idea makes you feel somewhat concerned—or, for that matter, if you feel a bit shaky about your references to begin with—you might think about supplying references that can be reached by mail only. For one thing, it is difficult to be enthusiastically negative in writing. This is partly because of the impersonal nature of written communication. Also, despite what they say about rain and snow and sleet not being able to stay the mailman from appointed rounds, the speed of the mails can surely dampen things. Finally, a busy reference might prefer a letter to the rigors of a phone interview or the immediate embarrassment of forgetting just who the heck you are.

Another word of advice. By all means, let your references know that they are your references. Tell them you are making use of their names. Even better, ask them if you may make use of their names and review your past associations with them. This helps avoid the situation of, "Berliner? Hmmmm, it does sound familiar—I just can't seem to remember much about him. Perhaps if you'll give me a couple of days to hunt in my files . . ." That's no good. Requesting your references' permission not only allows you to review your past accomplishments and revive their memories, it also brings you up a peg in the world of protocol.

Speaking of past associations, it is important to remember that there are implicit references hiding between the lines of your resume. Even though you may not explicitly mention them as references, your gang of former employers may very well be contacted to explain your relationships with their respective companies. Depending on the circumstances under which you left, I can easily imagine you shuddering at the thought. But, besides providing a good starting point for contacts, former bosses must be considered as implicit references. If your job history has been rough, you just may have to smooth out some of the bumps in your more rocky references. You never know when they might be contacted behind your back and provide whoever is asking with a veritable catalog of your lesser points. For guidance on how to carefully recycle your used (and abused) references, read the section in Chapter 3 entitled "Don't Overlook Your Former Employers."

An act of great kindness and consideration on your part is to be relatively stingy with your references. Don't give them out at the drop of a hat if you can possibly help it. As a first step, as I've already mentioned, wipe them off that resume; you don't want every Tom, Dick, and Harry calling up those valuable people. For that matter, you should hesitate revealing them in conversation, too. Good references are like fine recordings or a mint coin collection: you'd like to have people appreciate them, but not so often as to wear them out. You should be pretty far along in the job negotiation before offering those names. It helps to keep your recommendations in peak condition, ready to do their magic when you need them most.

But there is an additional, subtler reason: give out a name too frequently and the reference may start having horrible thoughts—about all the people you are talking to, about all the jobs you are interviewing for and, apparently, having trouble getting. Maybe you are not quite the guy he thought you were. And maybe his doubts will begin to show. The lesson is this: spare the reference; don't spoil your chances.

3 / Leads, Leads, Who's Got the Leads?

WITH your resume and references now ready and waiting, it's time to get down to business. You have to dig up some job leads and make the most of them. Generating leads is a key part of the job-hunting game, and there are many ways you can do it.

Playing the Ad Game

The most obvious and accessible source of job leads is the newspaper. We have been brought up with the idea that answering an advertisement is *the* prime way to seek out a new job. While it certainly doesn't hurt to scan the Sunday newspaper ads, you must do so in the right frame of mind. In simple terms, it just may take a while. You are not the only person searching through those ads. Many other people are scanning and answering them. It is not unusual for some box ads in the business sections of the larger newspapers to pull in several hundred responses. Furthermore, if you use the newspaper as your sole source of leads, you may not always be lucky enough to find the type of job you want. And if you do find the right ad, it may take some time before the company that placed it realizes it wants *you*. Assuming you are serious about wanting a job, time is valuable. You'll want to do more than just wait around for responses. You ought to be tapping other sources too. However, since newspaper ads are the most obvious source of leads, let's take a look at them first. A lot can be learned just by examining the ads closely. Beside the obvious—job description and company description (if published at all)—you should look between the lines of the advertisement to understand what is really being said.

Salary is a good place to start. It gives you an indication of the company's intentions. Many companies make you search through the ad for the salary figure printed in type equivalent to a whisper. You may even find that some companies just leave it out altogether. Although this may be unsettling, don't be discouraged. And don't lose a lead by skipping over these ads.

Through the years company ad writers have developed various ways to obscure the salary issue. For instance, an old favorite is "salary commensurate with experience." A company taking this approach is allowing itself a lot of leeway. It is really saying, "We don't know how much and what kind of experience we are looking for in a job candidate. Let's put the nets out and make sure we get a look at *everybody*."

Then there is the case when "compensation for this position is open." This company is not anxious to reveal its salary levels. The job description may seem irresistible, but the salary, if known, would scare everybody off. What if the compensation is "open and competitive"? That's a cute one. You may think this means they'll pay good bucks for talent, but perhaps the word "competitive" is meant to apply more to you than to them.

Still on salary, an employer might be looking for an "individual early in his/her career." That's a little less subtle. It sounds as though he wants people who simply haven't climbed very far up the salary ladder. You should be wary of employers who appear to be looking for bargains at a resume rummage sale.

If a company resorts to waving the extras out front—either "we offer a comprehensive benefits package" or "strong potential for advancement"—I back away, feeling very wary. I figure that Personnel is trying to lure me with the dessert because the main course isn't very appealing. Don't bite too fast.

Some companies may give you the impression they are more honest. No hushed tones here. They blare out the salary in bold face type for all to see. Did I say salary? I meant "salaries." A whole bunch of salaries is displayed in their ad. For example, "Salary—$1,220 to $1,450 per month." Now what does that mean?

The simple interpretation (which every so often still traps me) is that they are offering a starting salary somewhere between $1,220 and $1,450 per month. The exact sum will be determined later, based on the applicant's background, abilities, poise, and pluck as revealed in an interview. Well, that's simple enough. It's downright commendable for a company to lay out all the facts in plain sight.

Of course, almost everyone feels that he can use all his talent to shoot for that figure at the top end of the range. Wrong again! It's just not that straightforward. Believe me, I have fallen into the same trap several times. You must fill in the holes in that ad. You see, the salary range for this position is indeed what they have stated in the ad. The hitch is that the *starting* salary (which is what we're interested in) is actually a very specific figure in someone's mind. You will find out during one of your telephone contacts with the company (or, more likely, in the actual interview) that the starting salary is that specific figure, say, $1,300 per month. Your interviewer may go on to explain that the salary range mentioned in the ad is the *complete* salary range for the job. So, you feel let down in learning that you have no shot at starting at the upper end of the salary range and, worse, that strict salary constraints will be clamped on you for as long as you have that position.

Such ads are about as helpful as an automobile company claiming that its cars get "somewhere between 10 and 27 miles per gallon." Consumers (and surely the government) might just question that claim for more specifics. *Caveat emptor.*

There is of course the simpler phrase that appears all over the place—"salary *up to* $20,000." It is easy to skip right over those key words, "up to." Now, no doubt the job is only worth, realistically, about $15,000. However, an employer knows that an advertisement's dollar figure is a dreamer's pot of gold. Lots of ambitious dreamers making $10,000 are going to send their resumes in for a bid on this hot job in order to raise themselves up a notch or two. However, what the employer hopes to do is catch some of those actually making $15,000 at their present jobs with an "up to $20,000" net. He may even gather in a few $18,000, $19,000, or $20,000 fish in the same net. That would be an even better bargain. By merely "up-grading" the position in question, an employer can attract a higher level of respondents.

Two of the most mangled words that appear in job advertisements are "preferred" and "desirable." Who's kidding whom? In the old days, job hunters learned to shun the attractive "unlimited opportunity" or "no experience necessary." Nowadays, a company advertises that "an MBA with a strong concentration in analysis of balance of payments, benefits administration, and organizational concepts is *highly preferred but not necessary;* solid experience in financial analysis and controls, technological facilities planning, and information systems in a public utilities, banking, or retailing environment would be *desirable though not essential.*"

Why do employers bother to appear so open-minded? Don't they realize that an experienced job hunter gets the message? If you're weak in those "highly preferred" areas, you'll be fighting a real uphill battle to get that interview.

Often the ad describes "an unusual opportunity in a *highly visible position.*" Not only is this distracting, but its value as an extra is highly debatable. Do you really want someone peering over your shoulder, constantly hunting for your blunders?

Early in your search through the newspaper ad thicket you will quickly discover an annoying thorn: the blind ad. Here the company shamefacedly refuses to identify itself and asks you to reply to Box X4567 in care of a newspaper or some nondescript address.

This is an annoyance, but I am told there is some
logic behind it. That logic says that there are some
people scouring the job ads who will just jump when
they see a certain company name. Such a name will
often pull in a much greater number of responses
than the unnamed company, and some employers
would prefer not to wade through the resumes of all
those nonselective job seekers. Thus these companies
avoid placing ads that use their names or logos. They
run the blind ad so they don't have to identify themselves, although in an attempt to salvage just a wee bit
of that company name glamour, they may resort to
using the "Fortune 500 company in the Northeast"
bait to attract high-caliber applicants.

It's one thing for a company to desire anonymity.
But there is a worse situation you should know about:
Some blind ads are placed by organizations that have
no bona fide jobs to offer. Just think of the possibilities. People who answer employment ads willfully
submit all kinds of personal information to someone
they don't even know. Direct mail firms pay good
money for names of hot prospects and here is a way to
gather in a select group of individuals. I figure that
the invitation I received last month to invest in a
working chicken farm may very well have come my
way because of some innocent-looking blind ad I responded to some time ago.

But to return to the issue of advertisement word-
ing, I really don't want you to get the idea that every
ad is coldly thought out to discourage the inexperienced and tempt the talented. For instance, there is
the storybook ad, created by the copywriter with
the idyllic touch, beckoning you to enter the Emerald

City of Corporationville. The fairy tale is written with you as the central character, or so it seems . . . .

You went to school, graduated with that engineering degree, and went off to find your place in the tough world of manufacturing. How were you to know it wouldn't be your cup of tea? You liked the shirtsleeves involvement, sure, but still you knew your true interests lay elsewhere—the financial side of things. What can you do about it now?

With National Fairytales Corporation you will move directly into a position of financial responsibility and high visibility. Because of your thorough knowledge and strong experience in engineering technology and financial analysis and controls, management will look to you for realistic assessments of new product ventures from a marketing, financial, and technical viewpoint. What more could you ask?

You will find yourself in a lush country setting, conveniently located near a large metropolitan area. This, plus the satisfying feeling of working with other professionals with high standards and goals, makes your new, high-potential position in creative planning a real opportunity for growth, with a corporation that is experiencing continuous expansion.

Come join us. Discuss your possibilities with us any time this week over a cup of coffee. Call our Personnel Director—you'll be glad you did.

It sure makes a sweet-sounding story, but the copywriter may have gone a bit overboard. Don't be led too quickly down this yellow-brick road.

Playing Pinball

Going past the obvious and easy step of scanning
the Sunday papers, there are other more active things
you can do to generate job leads. One of the newer
but still lesser-known methods that seems to be getting around is the "pinball machine" approach. This
method sounds somewhat forced and is certainly
not for the timid, but it has some great things going
for it.

The idea is to "break into" an executive's office
somehow, not on the pretext of looking for a job, but
rather to get his "advice" and "recommendations."
The very fact that you come only to get his advice is
just flattering enough that you might get it. Because
he feels under no pressure to offer a job, he can be at
ease and speak honestly. You can take his advice and
use his referrals to bounce to the next executive, thus
obtaining further recommendations and keeping the
chain reaction going.

How do you "break into" an executive's office?
You can try breaking in cold, either over the phone or
in person (yes, in person). Several books recommend
this approach and go to great lengths to describe how
to dance around the "Who shall I say is calling?" receptionist and the "Is he expecting your call?" secretary, and how to hold the "breakee's" attention for
more than the twenty seconds he needs to decide
whether or not to cut you off.

Alternatively, you might warn your prospective
contact of your intention to visit. Although it may
seem like the cops calling the bank to warn the crooks,
it is useful to lay the groundwork with a letter and
resume a few days before you plan to call on your

executive. He then has a chance to digest your background a bit before being confronted by you. It's true that now he's also got a chance to reject you summarily before you meet him, but he would have asked for your resume sooner or later, and if he refuses to see you after reviewing it, well, you never would have made much headway anyway.

Of course, your introductory letter should never state directly that you are asking for a job or even for another referral. Remember, you are asking to meet the executive to "get his advice on your career plans for the future." Well, it might be smart to cover a few bases by inserting a modified form of "gimme a job." Without letting your tongue hang out in anticipation, you do want to make sure he knows that, if he *did* have a job in mind, you wouldn't be too averse to considering it. That's easily handled with a line like this: "While the possibility of joining your firm would be most exciting for me, there may naturally be no appropriate position open at this time." That takes the edge off nicely.

Shove a resume in with the letter and make a point of informing your soon-to-be-approached contact that you'll soon approach him in the next few days. Make sure you pave the way by telling him near the end of the letter, "I will be calling your office in the next few days for an appointment to discuss these matters briefly, at your convenience." And don't forget to follow up. Not that the executive will sit anxiously by the phone awaiting your call. However, your letter gives you a convenient wedge that ought to be used before it's worn out. That is, if you call a couple of days after your letter has been received, you can say with confidence to his secretary, "Hello, this is John Somebody. I would like to speak with Mr. Gabardine, please." Then drive in the wedge: "He's expecting my call." And you're in. You did say in the letter you were going to call, right? Once you get in to see your executive, you don't have any time to lose. As soon as you can, whip out another resume and ask him for some pointers on it. Did he like it, despise it, forget it, commit it to memory . . . what? Would he emphasize things differently, expand some items, reorganize, or cut down? You need some feedback on it. After this, he'll probably ask you to describe your background and working experience. Control yourself; remember, this isn't *This Is Your Life*. You are there to get his interest up, but also to hear him talk. You want to hear about his business, industry, profession, problems, and so forth. Then, when it is clear that it is time to go (take care not to overstay your welcome), you ask him who else you might speak to so you can keep your game in play.

As for the effectiveness of playing pinball, it certainly doesn't hurt to have made an impression on a few dozen business people. (And it doesn't hurt to leave a fresh copy of your resume on each desk.) Assuming you came across okay, each will file you away in the back of his mind. And when one hears of a job opening (in his own company or that of an associate elsewhere), whose name will pop up as the ambitious but sincere person who had the guts—and the intelligence—to come to talk to the executive about guiding his future? Well, it might be the person who tried the pinball machine route. ("Al told me you were looking for some sharp people to add to your department. I was speaking with this woman a few weeks ago, and she's really on the ball. I think you should see her.")

However, it is easy to go tilt if you try to rush things. There is the case of a guy who squeezed in appointments with executives during his lunch hours for a solid month. Besides running himself ragged (and never eating lunch), this person earned himself a reputation as a wishy-washy individual who seemed to be terribly unsure about his future directions and aspirations.

These stories quickly spread around the industry; but he still managed to get in to see the higher-ups despite all the tales. Despite them? No, because of them! Unbeknownst to our aggressive job seeker, he was breaking down all those doors because everyone felt sorry for him and felt he needed a guiding hand. They didn't want to hire him, just guide him. Should any demanding job lead come their way, they wouldn't dare route it through to this poor guy.

And his well-directed and well-organized resume didn't help either. Many of those who had heard the (exaggerated) stories about him never even bothered to give it a serious look. Those who did couldn't help noting the vast discrepancy between the poor lad and his success-oriented resume. They were downright appalled at what they surmised was a dishonest summary of his background. And so it went.

Looking at the brighter side, though, the most positive thing about playing pinball is that any referrals you do get are based on a face-to-face confrontation in which some executive has seen that you are a real human being, not just a faceless nobody with a nice resume. If you do get any further referrals, you can be fairly sure the executive is convinced there is good reason to give them to you. He likes something about you and wants to help you out. There is definitely something to be said for the personal contact that this approach brings into the job-hunting arena. A job search that mixes different techniques can also be successful. In attempting to finesse the pinball game, you will have had to make up a list of companies and/or executives that you want to see. Now, say you are having a *non*pinball-type interview (for a real job) that starts to go sour. Before the well completely dries up, quickly drag out your previously composed pinball list and ask your interviewer, "Do you think it would be a good idea to talk to Mr. So-and-So at the Acme Corporation?" or "Could you suggest some other people or companies I might talk with that would be more of a match for my interests and abilities?"

He might be a bit surprised, but since this is certainly a straightforward request, you might get some helpful leads. With his suggestions you can approach the next name on the list with a "Joe sent me" introduction that might make it easier to get your foot in the door.

One job-hunting book I saw recommends stretching the truth if necessary. You might encounter interviewers who are reticent about making suggestions and barely manage to grunt approval at your prospective list of future contacts. To utilize such minimal cooperation, all you have to do when attempting your next contact is to mention that "Joe Smith of the Benton Corporation agreed that I should get in touch with you." Who is going to spot the difference between "suggested" and "agreed"?

Don't Overlook Your Former Employers

In looking for leads, there is another group you should consider: your former employers. "This guy has really flipped," I hear you say. "How could I ever approach those people again? I was lucky enough to get out when I did." All right, just be patient and hear me out. There are some very good reasons why you should see your former employers.

The most obvious is that, whether you like it or not, your former bosses are fair game as references. Remember, as implicit references they are almost as important, and possibly more so, than the explicit references you supply upon request. The fact that you don't list the names of former employers on your resume is no guarantee that a prospective employer will ignore them. In truth, your deliberate omission of any former bosses from a bunch of references "supplied upon request" may be enough to arouse the interest of your would-be employers. They may then decide to dig out such unlisted but significant names from your past. Or you may be asked somewhere along the way, "Is there any reason you might not want us to contact a former employer?"

The second reason for visiting your former bosses is a more positive one. After all, you are the former employee of your former boss. Before you and he parted sweet company, the two of you had joined forces in the first place. He undoubtedly had decided at one time that you were good for the job. You had a certain something that he liked and wanted in his company. Why couldn't it happen again?

Assuming you parted under circumstances that

were largely beyond the control of both of you, the attraction could be lying dormant since your departure. And, if you parted under less than amiable circumstances, time may have healed the wounds. People will tend to forget about your faults and remember your strengths, especially if your replacement hasn't turned out so well. ("George, remember the great job Harry did on that complex Forbus acquisition project? I didn't give him enough credit at the time. He ran his people pretty hard, but I think the guy who replaced him takes things a little too easy.") So it's possible that a former boss's interest could be fired up easily by the same person who did it once before, namely you.

A very important reason for seeing a former boss is to smooth over old difficulties. If one of your previous employer–employee relationships ended under not so favorable circumstances, you'll want to patch up the crack by re-cementing the relationship. Your spackle is some experience the two of you shared. The trowel used to smooth it on is in the form of a short but nicely worded letter or warm telephone conversation.

As an example, let us assume that you quit a previous job because of a basic and occasionally bitter disagreement with your immediate boss over management style. Suppose one difference was that you tended to drive yourself, and anyone who worked closely with you, hard to meet a deadline or do that extra bit that you thought would polish up a report just the right way. You also felt that your boss, more easygoing perhaps, had too namby-pamby an approach in his dealings with the people who reported to him (including you). His viewpoint might very well have been that you were too abrasive for your own, or the company's, good and that his deceptively easygoing manner was the right way to really get things accomplished. To be fair, the situations that resulted probably always had at least two interpretations, but your viewpoint prevailed in your mind, and so you felt you had to leave that job.

Furthermore, suppose the straw that broke your boss's back was an angry confrontation between the two of you. In a burst of annoyance at his attitude, you lashed out at him and, among other things, insisted on a hefty raise as a reward for your hard-fought efforts on the latest project. And he, in his easygoing way, insisted you take your abrasiveness out of his office and out of the company. There you are, out on your ear, and not under the most pleasant of circumstances.

You can be sure that any prospective employer who stumbles upon this former boss for a reference will certainly get a detailed description of you. It won't be exactly the kind you'd appreciate, but detailed it will be. This could be disaster for you unless smoothed over by some careful efforts on your part.

"Smooth it over?" you say. "That guy wouldn't give me the time of day. How am I supposed to turn him into a positive reference?" It's easy; words can soothe the savage beast. And you don't have to be a hypocrite either. You could easily admit that you shouldn't have erupted and lashed out at him the way you did. When things get hot and heavy, most people say things they don't mean. So, rip off a letter to your former boss and explain just that.

Dear Frank:

I am considering leaving my present job and moving on to greener pastures. I just want to say that, in reviewing my past associations, it has become clear to me that you helped me out a great deal. Though our confrontations were often fiery, I think I learned much that I will never forget. That's true even for our last encounter, and I am thankful for that. Could I see you, perhaps sometime next week, to discuss briefly my future career plans? I would welcome your assistance and guidance.

Regards,

A little flattery like this can often work wonders. But you really don't have to say anything that's not true. By the way, what was the "lesson" that was learned? Who cares? The letter doesn't say and it really doesn't matter. The point is you can smooth things over while retaining your self-respect.

Also, with such a letter you can shift the burden of guilt onto your former boss. After reading it he'll think, "The guy really seemed to learn something. I wonder if I acted a little too quickly in firing him. I didn't like how he put it at the time, but maybe he did have a good point about my easygoing nature. He always seemed to get results from his associates, too." The doors open up, you and he spend a lovely hour together (free from the pressures of the employer–employee relationship), and you convert a negative reference into a glowing one and get three or four extra referrals as a bonus. That's the way to patch things up!

Hunting for More Leads

Let's move along to some other lead possibilities. Job-hunting happiness may mean exposing your background and warm personality to interviewers from several dozen companies in the span of a single day. I'm talking about the career conference in which you "Complete your job search in one afternoon. Meet with the companies of your choice. Select your career. Have on-the-spot interviews with any of the more than 100 recruiters from over 40 well-known companies."

I must say, though, that describing the feeling as "happiness" might be somewhat generous. Of course, under these particular conditions, you wouldn't expect in-depth interviews. And you may be ecstatic later if the session results in a fine position. But can you imagine the agony of enduring interview after interview all day long, ceasing only when you feel like crying out in pain at having to explain for the fourteenth time why you left your first job to take your second job or why you didn't do it soon enough?

Personally I feel that this is an utterly masochistic method of launching a job search. But I guess it is encouraging if you haven't filled your own quota of interviews lately. It will raise your batting average to undreamed-of heights. And maybe your blood pressure, too.

Another method of obtaining leads allows you to switch things around and really take matters into your own hands. Here you place your *own* advertisement and expose your talents and desires for all the world to see. Well, not exactly the entire world, just the particular segment that reads the newspaper or periodical you pick for placing your ad.

How effective is a "situation wanted" ad, anyway? A friend of mine insisted on trying it and ran a small box-number ad in the back of some professional journal. Amazingly, over the next week alone he collected seventeen responses to his plea for a "situation." He was ecstatic until he actually read the responses. Five of them were agencies (one executive search firm, two recruitment specialists, one "human resources" agency, and one placement organization) inviting my friend to use their services.

With less than overwhelming enthusiasm, I attempted to convince him that this response, such as it was, indicated the ad's ability to attract some kind of professional interest. But then he told me that four of the five agencies had previously had him in their clutches, had accomplished nothing for him, and had dropped from sight months ago. A sixth response was sent in by a firm specializing in resume preparation. They were sure they could improve his odds. He got four other letters from national franchise distributors anxiously inquiring if he were interested in plunking down some money on a local franchise that required no experience, needed a minimum investment of time, and rewarded you with an income far in excess of what you could earn at any ordinary job.

Three other responses were more closely related to the original intent of the ad but not quite on the beam. They were sent by other job hunters interested in trading leads obtained from similar personal ads that *they* had placed. One response came from a nationally known insurance company that wished to sell such an enterprising, up-and-coming young businessman a personalized insurance package that would guarantee him security and peace of mind in a single, complete financial plan. To top it off, my friend received one letter from a fellow who needed information for a book he was writing about the effectiveness of "situation wanted" ads.

In all fairness, though, two real-life companies responded with an invitation to talk things over. He called one of them and, in a moment when his guard was down, got forced into a modified telephone interview, and was turned down without further ado. A personal interview was obtained with the other corporate respondent. But my friend later discovered that this company was merely trying to squeeze out of him information to use in its trade war against his former company. All in all, placing the ad was not the most helpful experience.

Taking Aim with the Shotgun and the Rifle

A variation of the advertising approach, and one that seeks out its own appropriate audience, is the broadcast letter, often referred to as the shotgun approach. Essentially, you write a few different personal ads for yourself in a letter format, gather together a load of company names, perhaps hire a typing service to handle the details, and sit back and wait for the tidal wave of responses. But unless you're especially clever, that tidal wave will turn out to be more like a leaky faucet that keeps you up nights.

A better way of using a letter to generate leads is

to assemble a more specific type of broadcast letter—
the rifle. The rifle is used to zero in on a small number
of companies—maybe a half dozen—to which you can
write a special letter. By being specific you can compose a real powerhouse that shakes things up and
prods the recipients into action. Let's see how it goes.

> Mr. Arthur T. Sellum, President
> Whosis Wire and Cable Corporation
> Snippet, Wisconsin
>
> Dear Mr. Sellum:
>
> Speculation in the trade has it that you are seriously
> considering going nude.
>
> That is, a radical decision to strip away the two
> outer layers of your No. 8, 48-conductor, supercolloi-
> dal, coaxial hypercable and promote such a "nude"
> cable for underwater use is said to be a real possibility
> for your organization in the near future.
>
> Having worked at Rollem Cable and Wire for ten
> years, I have had a great deal of experience with both
> seminude conductors and the underwater applications
> involved (including the stripping, reclothing, mending,
> and difficult wearing operations). Over the last eight
> years I have succeeded in engineering several major
> breakthroughs in the cable field. I designed the outer
> jacket in which Rollem's corduroy cable is encased, and
> it was considered an innovation for the industry. This
> led to my work on supercolloidals and subsequently to
> seminudes.
>
> With the idea that your company is thinking of
> going strictly nude and the fact that I have been cam-
> paigning for this exciting concept for years, it strikes
> me that our association might make a very good union.
>
> I will call you early next week to arrange a time

when we can discuss our mutual interests and the ways in which I think I can contribute to your excellent, forward-looking firm.

Sincerely,

Okay, then. What are the basic ingredients of the rifle letter? First, *shock* your target. Knock him off the chair with the introduction. Then show the *relevance* of your letter. Throw in a problem or subject area that this industry should be concerned with. *Your relevance* to his problem should follow, and you should indicate some broad background that links you up with this company's business. *The perfect example* gives you a chance to strut out there with a few concrete facts that demonstrate your specific ability. But don't show everything; hold back a few things to encourage them to see you in person. Then bring it all to a close with *the line,* or a hint of admiration for the company; *the hook,* where you slip in, almost unnoticed, your desire for a job; and *the sinker,* telling your target that you'll be taking action soon. When you do call, he'll know who you are. Don't let him get away.

That's how the letter should go. Don't even include a resume; it would spoil the letter's impact. And when you send it out, stay away from the personnel department, personnel director, or anything of the sort. Personnel sees this stuff a hundred times a day and thinks nothing of depositing it in the usual circular receptacle. Instead, aim for the head of the department you would work in, or, if there are several possible departments, go right to the top and write to the president of the firm. Don't be satisfied with the title alone, use the person's name. Even if you were company president, wouldn't you be happier with a letter personally addressed to "A. T. Bigg, President" than with one saying merely "President"? And make sure the name is spelled correctly! If you are worried about getting your letter past some efficient secretarial roadblock, pick up a rubber stamp labeled "Personal and Confidential." Such a rubber-stamped declaration is notoriously seductive. If you have a few favorite companies, send your letters to them by certified mail or special delivery. That will get their attention. And if you suspect that hardly any outside communications ever penetrate your executive's suite, tramsmit your message via Western Union and hear those walls come tumbling down. Who can refuse a telegram? The telegram rams your foot in the door, and then you can follow up later with a conventional letter.

The shotgun and rifle approaches have a second cousin you can use if you aren't yet particularly fed up with your present situation. This is the backburner approach. Here you are saying, "I would just like to flash my credentials at you so that, should a job open up in the future, you would remember me and I could be considered for it." This letter obviously should not be as specific as the rifle example, nor should it quite knock the reader off his chair.

Since you don't want to come on like a juggernaut, your main point is brought out by some low-gear variation of this phrasing: "While I am very excited by the thought of eventually working for your firm, I am fully aware that a job opening may not exist at the moment. However, dynamic companies such as yours are always subject to change, and I am sure opportunities will arise in the future. One of these may well be a perfect match for the talents and experience I offer."

To ensure that you are indelibly inscribed in his memory, you should indicate you will be following up with a phone call to set up a personal interview. It is one way of getting him to sit up, open his eyes, and take notice.

Looking for a Job on the Job

If you are presently working, there is an interesting door to possible job leads which you can try to open. It should be done rather gingerly, however, because it is a loaded situation that can easily explode in your face. I am referring to on-the-job opportunities.

You may be unhappy with your present job, but the cause of your unhappiness may be the department, your particular boss, the particular tasks you are responsible for, or the particular people you have to work with. In any case, it doesn't mean you have to leave the comfortable company womb itself. By searching out job opportunities *within* your company you can change the scenery while sticking with the same act.

But it has to be done carefully. It is like answering a blind ad only to find out it was placed by the marketing manager of the product group down the hall from you. (Actually you could luck out even in that situation. The guy might not give a hoot that you're from within the company.) A better analogy is the blind ad you answer that was placed by your own boss or one of his longtime cronies. It pays to think out your moves when job hunting from within. It would be a shame to not only miss out on a good job opportunity but also create another one—your own.

Essentially there are two broad avenues of approach here—the aboveboard and the down-low (also called the under-the-table). With the aboveboard approach, you can avoid the embarrassment of having your boss inadvertently discover that you are out to liberate yourself from his clutches. You avoid this by the simple, yet often overlooked, mechanism of telling him. Yes, you undertake that heart-to-heart talk, detailing the source of your displeasure or discomfort. If he's willing to listen, then you make your pitch for freedom and perhaps indicate exactly what would make you happier within the organization.

The major plus for the aboveboard approach is the possibility that your solution may present itself right then and there. You or the boss may have needed a confrontation such as this to get things off your chest or his. One of you may discover qualities about the other that could be enlightening and, in fact, be a booster shot for your entire relationship. It might change the very aspects of your job that disturbed you in the first place. Wouldn't that be a pleasant turn of events?

There's only one obvious drawback: it very often doesn't work. It may destroy the rapport you do have with your boss and make things worse than they were. Most important, it doesn't get you that new job. Nothing compares with the wrath of a boss scorned.

Before dealing with the other alternative—the down-low—it should be noted that there is a back door variation of the aboveboard that an employee can use if he is looking at the long-term and not just the short-term hop. You might view it as sowing your oats properly to reap future crops. It is based on the fact that many companies have computerized their employee files and, in addition, require that updates be made periodically. Furthermore, many companies require that these files be searched before any candidate from outside the company is considered for a job opening. This sounds like quite a reasonable approach, doesn't it?

Well, it is, and it is probably followed right down to the letter of the requirement. But, to see what it results in, imagine for the moment that *you* are the employer. What would you do if, (1) you needed to hire someone; (2) your company required a search of all internal talent before going outside; and (3)—this is what sews it up—you just don't want to hire any of the stale bread from within the corporation when you can get a little fresh grain from the outside.

Put it all together, and it's a sure bet that you will fill out that employee requisition form in excruciating detail so you can eliminate any internal candidates from consideration for the position. With this maneuver you snip away all the red tape and hire someone from the outside, as you intended in the first place.

To make this plan work, the person with the job to fill must be very strict and all-inclusive in listing the desired qualifications and background the insider must have to fill the spot. Therefore you, the inside worker seeking a different job, must combat this by taking at least as much care in filling out the employee skills and background profile when hired, and you must update it as required. Pluck out of your personal resume collection the first one or two drafts you wrote—you know, the ones in which you enumerated in agonizing detail every aspect of your academic life, your employment story (from part-part-time to ultra-temporary), your extracurricular activities, and your special catalog of skills not always relevant to your present job.

Although you would never wish to include all these details in an effective resume (see Chapter 2), you need them in this situation. Here you must fill in the whole story of your life, covering as many bases as possible so you will be caught up in the fine-mesh computerized net of an internal search. The whole point is to try to outwit the guy who is hiring by having your background pop up as fitting his needs (contrary to what he expects or desires). Then, having made this contact, it is up to you to convince him in a personal interview that you are not the stale piece of bread he might have thought.

Now, as for the down-low or under-the-table alternative previously mentioned, it is very often the case that the riskier route has more valuable rewards. There is more risk in secretly attempting to sniff out a new job in your organization since, if your boss does find out, he may be terribly insulted at not being consulted and, even worse, he may be angry and vengeful. Depending on the particular political environment at your company, however, this may still be the more fruitful approach. You can take charge more directly than by relying on official contacts. You can buttonhole anyone in the hall who you think could help. This air of intrigue is sometimes more productive; other department heads' heads turn a bit quicker when they sense the opportunity to steal talent out from under a rival supervisor's nose.

The whole affair might even attract more interest than if the episode were sanctioned by your boss and choreographed by the personnel department. And, if you ever do find that better job, you can pat yourself on the back for having accomplished the switch all on your own with no help from your boss.

Of course, you'll have to be even more careful the next time you decide to hop. Because, knowing what you did to your former boss, your new boss will be watching you all the more carefully to ensure that you don't do the same to him. Every reward indeed has its own risk.

Remember Your Alma Mater, But Not Always Your Friends

Let's move on to another source of homegrown leads. If you went to college, chances are your alma mater offers job assistance of some sort, usually through a placement office.

This service can vary greatly in quality, of course. There are the schools that really offer it in name only in order to bolster the floundering level of "excellence" that their catalog declares is a "way of life at Storyville U." Off in a dusty wing long overdue for renovation, the S.U. job placement office sits like an old spiderweb, content to remain undisturbed forever. Inside are an assortment of U.S. Government Printing Office pamphlets pathetically describing various occupations ("So You Want to Be an Accountant . . ."); a collection of overblown company literature produced by all the large and medium-size corporations and guaranteed to leave you glossy-eyed

("Let your future be ours! Mechanico is on the go!"); the badly reproduced list of civil service tests given by federal, state, and local governments (some careless assistant invariably staples the second sheet upside down on the bulletin board); and the never-ending armed forces recruitment information ("Take a job with the Army. Where else can you get 30 days paid leave the first year?"). The place is not really set up to do more than leave you with a vague notion of what kinds of jobs and companies exist.

The superior college placement office takes much greater pains to help a candidate find a job. It has personnel trained in seeking out actual job openings with companies, assisting people in putting together effective resumes, offering suggestions on how to handle an interview. It maintains files of companies and contacts in those companies; it encourages companies to use its facilities for purposes of interviewing; and it tries to convince successful alumni to use the services of the placement office in the future when, as employers, they can help fellow alumni who will follow in years to come.

Although the role of the college placement office is similar to that of a private placement firm (see Chapter 4), the actual interviews and interactions that take place could not be more different. The people in good college placement offices will always back you to the hilt in your aspirations and strongly urge you to branch out even beyond the confines of your original college major. ("I know you're a philosophy major, but that shouldn't stop you from pursuing that newspaper job.") Their imagination knows no bounds, and they encourage you along any path you wish to pursue. It is a joy to encounter such optimistic and imaginative people, mainly because it does wonders for your ego.

Unfortunately, though, it can lull you into a fairy-tale stupor. You have to watch out for some of those misty-eyed dreamers in the placement office because they'll send you after the stars. It's not that they are trying to lead you astray. It's just that, unlike the private placement agency, the college placement office is not in the market for money. So they don't really care how long it takes you to find *the* job. They are merely offering a service for which alumni have been screaming for years. Just the very existence of the office is considered an accomplishment.

The thing you must remember here is that college placement counselors have no direct financial stake in your success at getting a job. Coupled with the idealistic bent of many colleges and universities, this creates a cushy atmosphere that can easily send you floating. But it may inadvertently do more harm than good, for you can get sidetracked. So if you do use your alma mater's placement office, force yourself to retain strict control of your senses. Sure, you can good-naturedly accept their advice, but it doesn't mean you have to follow it.

Another unfortunate aspect of college placement services centers on the usually lopsided logistics involved. Since it is readily available, easy to use, and free, many alumni and undergraduates use their college's placement office. The surroundings are familiar, the staff is very eager to help, and there are none of the pressures you find in a company or even an agency relationship. It also takes no great skill for a job candidate to pore over a listing of job openings periodically sent to him by the placement office.

Although most of the same congenial and conducive conditions prevail from an employer's point of view, there are far fewer employers than candidates registering with college placement offices. At first glance, you would think that companies would find the terms enticing enough to use the service. But this isn't the case, because, as far as the companies are concerned, there is just no selectivity. Anyone and his uncle can register with a college office and peruse the job listings. And almost everyone is enthusiastically encouraged to go after most of the jobs available.

This is why so many employers, despite the attractive price and the encouragement given by the placement office, shy away and instead hire a private agency (either on retainer or commission). They'd rather skim the cream off the top than wade through all the homogenized Grade C stuff.

Digging down into the bottom of the barrel of possible leads, I feel compelled to put in a word for personal contacts, that is, friends, relatives, and acquaintances. The word is *don't!* Accept some advice, cultivate a reference, use a third-party approach and ask a friend to answer a blind ad, but don't embarrass everyone concerned by squeezing a contact out of an acquaintance. Often the intermediary hasn't even any idea what you or the contact does for a living. And the guy who agrees to interview you is doing it only as a favor to your acquaintance. After a short chat, it becomes clear that your experience and interests and his needs are the mismatch of the century. Realizing this, he confesses he cannot help you. Then he attempts a minor resurrection by insisting you call him if there is anything at all he can do for you, anything at all.

Back to the Newspaper

One last type of lead that you can scout on your own is a variation of the shotgun approach (described earlier), but somewhat more discriminating in its aim. Rather than spraying letters out in all directions, this approach aims for more specificity. The idea is to scan your newspaper columns for news of "Business People on the Move" or some such heading. This is where the papers place reports on the shifts that occur in the corporate world—upward, outward, and, occasionally (in a well-disguised way), even downward. It is felt that this is an instant source of possible leads. Also, the particular job switch described gives you a great lead-in when composing your initial contact letter. Again, as in the usual broadcast letter, you will want to come up with an angle for presenting yourself.

An example is in order. Let us say you spotted this item in the business section of the newspaper:

> Thomas Gilbert has recently been named to head the Business Opportunities Division of National Sprocket and Spindle. This division will seek out new application areas for the firm's main products. Gilbert was previously in charge of marketing for the company's Eastern region.

Before jumping in headfirst, it is important to do a little between-the-lines translation at the outset. This firm is in trouble, and, fortunately, management realizes it. New business opportunities have to be identified and developed, so a new group has been started up. They need a dynamic leader and organizer with a marketing orientation to come in and shake up things. Up-and-coming Gilbert is their man. But Gilbert the marketing man is going to need some qualified talent to assist him. Let's see how we might communicate effectively with Gilbert on the matter at hand.

> Dear Mr. Gilbert:
>
>   Congratulations on your recent move up in National's organization! I am sure your performance as the Eastern region's marketing manager fully warrants assuming this challenging new responsibility.
>
>   The obvious advantage in moving a person like yourself into this new position lies in the immediate applicability of your experience in marketing. After all, a business opportunities group must have a person at the helm who is keenly aware of how to evaluate new markets for existing products.
>
>   To complement your well-honed marketing talents, you will probably want to consider adding strong financial skills to your team. Realizing that you are a busy man about to take on increased responsibilities, I have enclosed a capsule summary of my background, which I believe could mesh well with yours.
>
>   Please just take a moment to scan the relevant points. To expedite matters, I will give you a call early next week so we can discuss this matter more fully.
>
>   Sincerely,

This letter was built around a candidate's background that complemented Gilbert's obvious marketing leanings. However, a person strong on the marketing side could, with a few minor changes, just as easily aim to supplement Gilbert's background rather than complement it. In any case, for this type of letter you use the job change as the obvious point of departure, with a mild compliment to the promotee. Next you exploit the other particulars mentioned in the news blurb (plus whatever had to be interpolated) and set the reader up by focusing on one of his obviously strong attributes. Then present yourself as the logical, natural complement or supplement to him, and while noting what a busy time of life it must be for him, explain the action you plan to take. Crisp, neat, and logical—that's what it is all about.

The only drawback to this scheme is that you must find a news announcement that describes a person (or department) you feel you would want to work with (or in). The nice part is that, once you find it, you have at your fingertips all those reported facts around which you can construct a letter. There is more direction and control here than in many other job-lead situations.

Of course there are cautions, too. You want to avoid the executive who has either been moved laterally or pushed up in the organization because he is a poor manager. Often this is difficult to discern. The announcements never come out and say: "Garrison, Gear, and Gantry has announced that Roger Niblet is being relieved of his duties as Director of Operations after only six months on the job because of his overall managerial incompetence. . . . He has been appointed chairman of a newly formed task force on manufacturing operations created to provide a relatively harmless slot in which to shove him." You can only learn this by looking into the firm's background via other information such as other announcements or contacts in the industry, or through selective reading between the lines. For instance, any "newly formed task force" is probably a dangerous area in itself. Task forces are often used to hide away less effective personnel and are mostly temporary anyway.

Perhaps an easier situation to handle with this approach is the intercompany move. Although two companies are now involved, it is more likely that the job-hopper is going on to a better situation. Use the same tactic and try hopping after the executive; there's nothing wrong with spreading some of the wealth around.

4 / Job Leads Through the Middlemen

or

How the Agencies Give You the Business

THERE is another source of job leads many people have explored and would rather forget. This is the middleman—also known as the employment agency, personnel agency, recruitment specialist, placement organization, and the like. I'd like to use the catchall term "agency" here, even though these middlemen may not like it. For them to think of their company as a mere employment agency would, no doubt, cause their egos to wither away. They, of all people, know what it means to have an image, yet the image many people have of them is pretty low. However, agency is a convenient term, so let's use it.

How the Agency Game Works

There I was, waiting in the reception area of an agency barely two days after mailing my letter and resume in answer to an ad phrased in generalities.

Why this blinding speed? Because I was dealing with an agency, not the slow-to-move personnel department of some company.

This is the most obvious characteristic of an agency. To put it simply, once you send in your letter, the agency contacts you either immediately or not at all. I suppose that in their business they have to make extremely rapid judgments. Since an agency's income depends on the number of people it can place, it can't waste time weighing things such as your talents too long. Quick decisions are the name of the game. The individual using an agency needs a powerhouse resume that will present him immediately as a warm, tempting "placeable." So whether or not an agency calls you is great feedback on the effectiveness of your resume. For if they call you at all, rest assured that by the time someone interviews you, he or she will have studied your resume in great detail and will have digested all the important facts of your life and accomplishments.

After waiting for what seems like three seconds in the tastefully furnished (contemporary but not ultra-modern) waiting room, one of the agency's personnel/recruitment/placement specialists bounds in, greets me warmly, and leads me back to his office. He begins with a lot of small talk, for several good reasons. First, he wants to put me at ease, since the agency likes a happy candidate. Second, he wants to see how I generally handle myself in an interview situation. And third, since I am there seeking not one particular job but any of a number he has on file, he cannot really talk about a specific job yet. Fourth, and not least, his decision to pursue my case depends on my not having three eyeballs or an unfortunate habit, like clipping my nails during an interview.

The interview itself may be a mixture of several basic types, but the difference from a company personnel interview is that once you pass, you are in. It is not necessary to return for a second or third interview. But before you start dancing in the streets over this revelation, you should keep in mind that this is just the beginning of a long climb. Remember that there are company interviews you will have to undergo. And, as will be described later, you can be just as quickly *out* of the agency's graces as in.

Anyway, eventually my interviewer comes to the part where he is supposed to, as they say, "pinpoint my interests and experience," so he can match me with one of the myriad job openings in the agency's files. The "pinpointing" went something like this:

Interviewer: I see you have strong experience in bookkeeping that you did for a local repair shop. We have a firm that needs an analyst to design some financial systems for eventual computerization. Do you think you can handle that?

I: Well, I don't know if it is all that related to my background. Besides, that was just a summer job. I was thinking of something more . . .

Interviewer: . . . in the line of market research perhaps? I noticed your background in consumer testing. One of our bank clients needs someone to start up a market research function for them. How about that?

I: I am not really oriented that way. I do my best work in . . .

Interviewer: . . . in straight engineering, probably. You do have a bachelor's degree in mechanical engineering. Perhaps you'd be more suited for our pharmaceutical client

who needs some basic production machin-
ery design for a new product line.

I: But I haven't done engineering work since
college.

And so it went. He kept seizing upon details in my
resume that bore any relationship at all to a job in his
assorted files, and I constantly tried to make his and
my life easier by merely telling him what I wanted to
do. After I finally told him what kind of job I had in
mind, he admitted, in a burst of courage, what I'd
suspected almost from the beginning: "In all honesty,
we don't have anything like that. But the moment
something in that vein pops up, I'll be in touch with
you." And I never heard from him again.

Obviously agencies can only offer interviews for
whatever jobs they have in stock. If none of these
matches the agency's assessment of your background,
you're out of luck. They're not going to hunt up the
right thing for you. After all, since most agencies
work under a "fee paid" arrangement (the company
pays the fee), it's the party paying the bills who gets to
call the shots. The agency is really working for the
company, not you. With that allegiance, it is surely
better for the agency to keep the company happy
than you. In short, the agency knows on which side its
bread is buttered.

Now, after the interview, you'll have to wait until
you hear from the agency again, and this may be one
day or five months. On top of that, one week may
bring in three leads and the next month a big fat zero.
These uneven results are due to the "grass is greener"
attitude of personnel placement—the tendency to go
for something new and a little different. If a ripe new
candidate walks through the agency's doors, your

superb but, by now, familiar background is soon forgotten. Let's face it, agencies have short memories. If you want to keep their interest piqued, it's a good idea to give each of your agencies a brief call periodically or send a short note. You don't need any special reason. Keeping them interested is reason enough.

Some real enthusiasts go out of their way to compose a new resume every so often. They shorten some descriptions, reword this talent, reemphasize that accomplishment, rearrange some companies—in short, they give themselves that "new look." Then they send copies to their agencies and, for that matter, to any company they've had contact with during the last couple of months. It's like buying a new suit or getting a haircut; it gives you that new look and perhaps some renewed confidence in continuing your hunt.

Other Agency Ploys That Keep You on the Hook

In all fairness, one agency does not a generalization make. There are some that don't even bring it to the interview stage. A few days after answering an ad, you may receive in the mail the "I am sorry this reply could not have been more personal but . . ." letter with an attached application form that must be filled in before you can be referred to any client company. This is the "plantation approach." Agencies plant a bunch of advertisement "seeds" to harvest a ready crop of resumes. A new agency might resort to this method to impress future client companies with their swiftly garnered roster of qualified candidates.

I guess the most annoying thing here is the lack of communication one usually has with an agency like this. It might be months upon months before you receive any encouraging word. And, if you happen to specialize in an area the agency doesn't deal with, months and months might turn into years and years. Your telephone calls bring no satisfying answers either. The unkindest cut of all comes in the form of another "I am sorry, etc." letter that gets sent out as the result of some agency VP's edict to weed out their bulging files. With no date indicated at the top, and perhaps no trace of your name appearing anywhere, the note zooms right into the meat of things.

Please pardon this form of response, which we have chosen so that we may devote more attention to placing our applicants in lucrative positions. Having received your resume some time ago, we would like to confirm if you are still seeking a change of employment. If you would just take a few moments to complete the form at the bottom of this sheet, your cooperation will be very much appreciated.

Sincerely yours,

Robert Chesler

President
Management Unlimited

_____ I am still seeking employment. Please continue sending your career newsletter.

_____ I have taken a job with _____ .

                                    Position _____

                                    Salary   _____

_____ I would like to work with Management Unlimited in placing applicants with my new company.

_____ I am no longer actively seeking another job.

_____ Other_____

"Management Unlimited? Who could that be?" I usually murmur after receiving one of these letters. No doubt if I search my files I'll find buried in the stack of advertisement responses a faded Management Unlimited clip. One such agency was so efficient in its file-cleaning that as March of every year rolled around, the mail would bring, like an out-of-phase Christmas card, another "update" letter of this kind. Though I suppose it was nice to know they still had me on file, it was somewhat disconcerting to be updated but never informed of a job opening. After two years of pardoning them for their useless response, I finally decided I'd had enough. I sent back the form saying I had taken a job with Executives Incorporated, a well-known agency and competitor of Management Unlimited. I knew that would take care of them.

Do You Really Need an Agency?

One interesting thing may occur soon after you begin obtaining job interviews through agencies. You'll probably have continued keeping an eye on the newspaper advertisements, and it may happen that soon after a particular job interview, you'll spot an ad that has a familiar look to it. It describes precisely the company and position for which you just interviewed! The company's name may be explicitly mentioned, but even if it is not, you can identify it from unmistakable clues in the ad. If this should happen to you, you'll probably have a few depressing thoughts. "Was the company so unimpressed with me that they felt they had to repeat the ad immediately?" you ask, or, "What do I need an agency for in the first place?"

If you find yourself asking the first question, just bear in mind that the only reason the ad showed up at all is that the company, at least before speaking to you, merely planned to leave no stone unturned in seeking qualified candidates for the responsible and important position. Besides, the ad may have appeared after your meeting only because of the lead time the newspaper required to plan its Sunday edition or because of the company's personnel department did not cancel the ad in time.

As for the second question, whether you need an agency in the first place, the answer depends on several factors. The most important is the status of your present employment. If you are *not* working while seeking employment, don't go out of your way to look for an agency's help. It's not that they don't want to help unemployed people find new jobs. It just so happens that unemployed (I prefer "interjob") people are usually considered invisible or at least nonmarketable.

This is due to a deep-seated bias that "working is wonderful; unemployed is ugly," or something to that effect. I guess the agencies think you probably left an employer under nasty circumstances and, worse yet, that you might pull that trick again. Agencies get more satisfaction out of helping an employed person give his two-week notice to seize another job. So remember the basic creed: "Agencies avoid, if unemployed."

If you are working but want another job, you must face the fact that certain job openings will never be advertised in the newspaper but will be handled only by agencies. If you intend to use company ads as the sole alternative to working with agencies, it might be wise to rethink that decision. You need alternative methods of generating job leads if you want to do without agencies.

There is one other catch about the agency game that should be mentioned here. In dealing with agencies, you can't express more than a slight interest in changing jobs or show too much enthusiasm in volunteering your availability. Otherwise their desire for you will dwindle catastrophically. Don't be overanxious. Maintain an air of interested disinterest. One of my (presently working) associates never bothers contacting his former agencies at all and claims that some of them just eat this up and desperately try to reach him periodically. I always wonder what the conversation must be like: "Hi, Mr. Willis. We heard you weren't in the market for a job. We think we've got just the thing you're not looking for."

Then there is the larger issue of using agencies in general. In the job-hunting process, the agency is often described as a filter necessary to refine the flow between candidate and company. Many agencies, however, have a reputation of either vastly overdoing or underdoing this. You must realize that whatever method they use can affect your chances in getting interviews and, more important, employment.

Some agencies take the "sponge mop" approach. They just soak up all the potential candidates they can and wring them out all over the employment countryside. Candidates are quickly interviewed (sometimes not even in person), resumes are printed up in wholesale quantities, phone calls are made, and letters sent in blitz proportions to keep company contacts alive. Efforts are made to speed up the decisions of companies and candidates alike. At first the sponge-mop approach is very encouraging. Both candidates and companies are pleased with the volume of activity. But it soon becomes apparent that quantity of activity cannot take the place of quality of job/candidate matches.

Then there is the opposite approach, the "eyedropper." Some agencies dam off the flood of applicants to a piddling few drops. They feel that, with all those candidates out there, they may as well forward only a select few to their client company. (Why waste everyone's valuable time with an applicant who only has *potential* in a certain area?)

Once again, these selective agencies are initially regarded very highly. "They are not wasting my time with unqualified applicants or uncertain resumes," thinks the delighted company client. Likewise, the impressed candidate hums, "They are not wasting my time sending me on unproductive interviews."

Alas, it becomes only too clear that, in many cases, the eyedropper agencies are using the wrong mixture in the wrong eyes. They keep missing the target because they often don't quite know what it is they are selecting or what they are selecting for. It seems that either approach—sponge mop or eyedropper— needs only to make a match or cultivate a contact just often enough to keep the clients hungry and jumping.

As with any relationship, eventually the time comes to say good-bye. Breaking off relations with an agency is often not very difficult. After all, you don't have to worry about the ones that have been mummified into inaction because their jobs don't match your talents, their interests don't match your interests (I'll say), or their VP doesn't like your looks. However, when you start getting that update questionnaire after months and months of silence, just send it back with "still looking" checked anyway. You've got nothing to lose, and besides, next year (when the next questionnaire comes around), you may be looking for another job.

The tough ones to say good-bye to are the middlemen who were really close to you in spirit and action, even though they didn't get you the job you actually took. It is like an extended summer romance: the relationship was great, but your life has changed and you have other things to do and other places to go. However, you may need the relationship sometime in the future, so be discreet about ending it now.

You don't have to bother devising a way to kiss off the agency that did get you the job. They know they did you a favor. Your side of the relationship may fizzle, but they've got their hooks into you for good.

As a child wandering around the downtown streets of a metropolis, I always used to wonder how so many bars, barber shops, or laundromats in a ten-block area could all do well enough to stay in business. You may have been thinking the same thing about employment agencies now, and the explanation is very similar. There are enough customers for everyone. An agency needs a basic core of contacts, and there are enough new clients born every minute to keep the doors opening. And that's the name of the agency game.

5 / Pre-Interview Game Plans

YOU need to turn your job leads into job interviews if you want to move ahead in the job-hunt game. Here is where an advertising background would really come in handy. After all, can writing copy for a soft drink be that much different from writing copy about yourself? This is what your pre-interview correspondence is all about.

The Ins and Outs of Writing Cover Letters

After your resume, one of the next important pieces of writing you may face is the lead letter sent in response to some advertisement.

Is a letter really necessary? you may ask. Should you send a resume without a cover letter? This depends on how impressive your resume looks. Does it scream out to be read? How general or specific is it? Most important, how relevant is your resume to the job advertised? If you've had a pro compose it for you, you might be inclined to leave out your own letter entirely. Even so, there are reasons to consider including one anyway.

If the resume has been composed in a very general way, a cover letter will certainly help pin it down to the specific job under consideration. And a cover letter lets the company know you think of it in personal terms, not as a huge, multinational, hierarchical, billion-dollar corporation. They really can appreciate this bit of personalization. For this very reason, don't miss the point (and the job boat) by photocopying, mimeographing, printing, or otherwise duplicating cover letters. If you wonder why, just recall how it feels to receive one of those Xeroxed rejection letters (with your name typed in or, even more devastating, of the "Dear Applicant" sort). You don't want to hurt your prospective employer's feelings, do you?

There is another side to the dilemma. Should you send a cover letter without a resume—sort of an "uncover" letter? Again this depends on how impressive your resume looks. If there are certain unhappy things you felt you had to include in your resume, well, forget the resume and write out a letter that will do you right! Mention the relevant accomplishments, use appropriate names when they help (schools, companies, and so on), and throw in the time factor where possible (". . . worked at Marvel, Inc., for four productive years"). The best thing about composing an uncover letter is that you call the shots—you alone decide what to include and what to omit, what to emphasize and what to play down. There is just no standard format for an uncover letter. You might call it a formless resume.

Assuming you are answering an ad, the next problem is to whom to address the letter. This isn't as simple as it sounds. Did you ever write a letter to Mr. ZO19ST? It's not an earthshattering problem, but it can temporarily throw you the first time around. In many advertisements, companies provide only a box number or, in a moment of carelessness, perhaps a "Vice President, Employment" with a box number. Should you write to "Dear Vice President," or "Dear VP"? And if no title is given, is it "Dear Sir" or "Dear Madam," or should you cover all bases with "Dear Sir, Madam, Miss, or Ms."? What about "To Whom It May Concern"?

I used to stick with "Dear Sir" until I realized that, even though there aren't large numbers of women in the executive suites, they still do tend to monopolize the secretarial ranks. Who do you think is going to slit open the countless applicants' envelopes and be the first to lay eyes on that salutation of yours? It may be a secretary who determines your fate from the very beginning. In some organizations, the secretaries are really the ones who keep the organization running smoothly anyway. So don't rile them by throwing in an inappropriate "Dear Sir."

For the majority of cases where no name is given, I have adjusted my style and now prefer "Dear Department Manager." In this way, even if you may have mislabeled the title, you have still specified exactly one person, and that person happens to be anyone reading the letter! Better to have mislabeled than never to have labeled at all.

Even if a name is revealed in an ad, things are not necessarily simplified. I refer to the sneaky ad that requests you write to a "G. Washington." Personnel is really testing your ingenuity on this one. Though sheer odds would suggest a male, what if a woman is hiding behind that "G"? I imagine most women would be more upset at receiving a "Dear Mr. Washington" than just a "Dear Sir." And to complicate the issue even further, some women are just as turned off by a "Ms." as are many men. Compromise seems to be the best route here. Given them a "G. Washington" up there with the company name and address, and slip in a "Dear Sir or Madam" in the salutation. Personalized but inoffensive—that's the way to do it!

Now you need an opening for your letter. You just announce at the very beginning your intention of applying for the specific job mentioned in the ad, right? Wrong! There is nothing more dull and unprovocative than the standard opening, "I would like to apply for the job of chemical engineer that was advertised in the business section of the Sunday Picayune-Herald on January 12." It is not only uninteresting; it's downright unnecessary. The company certainly knows it placed the ad and doesn't need the reminder, so don't waste that prominent first sentence. After all, with three, four, or five hundred others out there pushing for the same job, this letter is your chance to attract attention and make an impression—*fast.* You can't pussyfoot around, even for a sentence, or you may be passed over for the next applicant.

An excellent way of starting a letter is to use the humble chest-pounder opening. March out one or two characteristics of yours that really fill the bill, dress them up tastefully, and let them parade forcefully before the reviewing stand. "My training in solar oven construction, my background in geological science, and my experience in rural living should stand me in good stead for the position you advertise." Note how once you have struck, it is easy to slip in mention of the job advertisement almost as an afterthought.

Of course, there is more than one way to grab attention. Some people believe that the chest-pounder is too immodest. An attention-getting alternative is the "spotlight." Flash a bright saying and then work yourself quickly into the spotlight.

> Who said, "A stitch in time saves *nine*"? Whoever did, it was a poor guess at the limits to which cost cutting can be extended. As an industrial engineer at United Forklift, I instituted workflow procedures that increased productivity by a factor of *nine and a half*. And I can create similar savings for you in the position you advertise.

Other more specialized openings almost always involve a unique approach tailored to the kind of job you are hunting for. An ad copywriter seeking a new position might package his pitch as a sample advertising message with himself as the promotable product. A reporter aspiring to change jobs could cover his own story in the style of the particular newspaper he is writing to, complete with headline, subheadings, plot, and commentary. The trick is to use a format that will appeal to others in your field.

No doubt some of you are protesting that these suggestions are terrific devices to use only if you are hunting in a field where such specialized approaches are appreciated. To use these approaches, you may say, you must have something to scream about. But even if your experience is minimal, you can still use a neon sign. You just have to display a different message. Write a beautiful love song that will capture the reader's heart (and an interview invitation). Use your intense interest in the firm, the position, or the firm's product to derive your eye-opener.

> As far back as I can remember, I have always wanted to further the growth of the lighting industry by pushing for beneficial legislation as a lobbyist for the National Association of Lamp and Chandelier Manufacturers. I have long been fascinated with the fantastically wide assortment of lamps and chandeliers manufactured in this country. Thus, I made a special effort to memorize the detailed design of every new lighting device I came across. This has enabled me to recognize the intrinsic worth . . .

And so on. It *is* possible to forge great enthusiasm and desire into a very positive lead-in in order to interest the prospective employer.

There is a key point to remember in any opening. For that matter, it should be applied throughout the letter and in general serve as an organizing principle through your entire job campaign. It is this: always emphasize "here is what I can do for you" rather than "this is what you can do for me."

As a prospective employer, which of the following sounds more attractive? "You can use my special background in heat-impervious plastics to upgrade your corporate research program," or "I am most anxious to seize this opportunity to broaden my background in managing research personnel." The difference is obvious when the two cases are put side by side, but it is amazing how many experienced as well as inexperienced people make the mistake of thinking inwards rather than outwards.

Okay, if you haven't done so already, now is the

time for the come-on—that tantalizing hint of your background, the mere wisp of a suggestion that what you have is just what they want. You're really performing a striptease on paper, and you should try to give some proof of your claims. But you can't give too much away because you want to keep them reading. Depending on your particular background you might want to toss off a degree or two, or a job experience, or a college name. If you didn't include a resume, you'll probably have to include a little extra information to hold their attention.

The striptease analogy fails, however, when applied to the entire letter. In the job-search arena it's all business; the customers do not want to be tantalized for too long, or they'll turn to others. So keep it on the short side, particularly if you are enclosing your resume. Then, wrap up the show with a "why don't you come up and see me sometime" hint (though not, of course, with those exact words).

You're almost finished now. But before you close that letter, it's a good idea to read the advertisement again—carefully. The company may request specific things they want you to include in your letter or resume. Standard items are salary history and requirements, geographic preference, travel restrictions, job title (several jobs may be advertised by the same company), and perhaps some written example of your work (as if the letter itself weren't enough). One firm even had me send a copy of their own ad with my letter of application.

The question of whether to mention your salary history or requirements is a hotly debated issue in the job-hunt business. If you do so, you may be conceding too much to your "opponent" too early in the game.

Some advisers insist you should avoid the subject like the plague at this point in the game. They claim it is best to completely ignore such requests and not reveal a bit of your salary background for fear of undermining your later bargaining position.

On the other hand, one can argue that it is the company's ad you are answering, that they really do want all of the information they are asking for, and thus, that it may be necessary to comply strictly with the numerous terms of the advertisement if you want to get past the first step in the selection process. In this situation, you can't make much use of your persuasion or evasion abilities. The letter medium has a certain finality to it.

Of course, each case must be examined individually before deciding whether to include the salary information. But in general, the most reasonable solution is the good old reliable compromise. Handle it the same way you would if asked the salary question early in an interview. There, you'd put off the issue by suggesting a salary *range*. In the letter-writing situation it is even more appropriate. You appear to be fulfilling the advertisement's requests and thus cannot be tossed into the reject pile. And, if you feel you must describe your "complete salary history," give them just enough to whiz your letter through the filtering process; say "low teens" or "middle teens," or just plain old "teens," depending on what your past salaries were. (I know it is tempting to say "salary in the five-figure range," but that comes off as downright evasive.)

Anyway, the basic point was to read the ad carefully, just in case you left out something significant. And don't give them anything they didn't ask for.

Like a good soldier, listen to orders and don't volunteer. Except for one thing. Although it is never stated explicitly in an ad, companies want to know about your future plans, so you might want to give them some idea of your career goals. As in your resume, this is a good way to pull your background together and orient your prospective employer in the right direction. Try to get across why and how you think this job will contribute to your future aspirations, how everything you have done in the past has been leading up to it, and how you feel that the marriage of this job and your mind will be the best match to come along in a while. But do it in one sentence; you don't want this getting out of hand. Remember, brevity is a virtue.

In planning the overall tone of your letter, some job-hunt experts point out that the first person who reads it and decides whether it goes into the "Possible" or "Forget It" piles probably will not be well acquainted with the position advertised. Apparently the underlings who leaf through the resume stack are often given only a superficial description of the characteristics for which the responses should be scanned. Thus some cover letter experts think you should make the letter as simple as possible. Their advice is to charge in fast with a ready sword.

Dear Sirs:

You advertise for someone who can slay fire-breathing dragons, rescue lovely damsels from danger, handle noble steeds with ease, and doesn't mind wearing metal pants all day. I do every one of these things. As the enclosed resume indicates, I also have had five years experience dealing with kings, and three years repairing castle walls. I am the knight you need. Let's get together for an interview.

I think this approach is too much of a gamble. What if you make it past the important first step and sway the underling reader? Then the man or woman who is actually doing the hiring or the person you would be working with will see your letter. It would be a pity to earn applause in the first act only to be laughed off the stage before intermission. Thus your letter should be short and to the point but also broad enough to appeal to several audiences.

Finally, in closing the letter, you probably should let them know you would be glad to hear from them soon (one can't assume anything these days). It's a convenient way to end the letter, and it lets you reemphasize your interest in the position and in winning an interview. This *is* what it's all about. As for the actual closing phrase, don't get hung up on whether you're writing this letter "sincerely" or "cordially" or "very truly." It's not something to worry about. Just keep the business letter atmosphere.

Hiding behind a Third Party

In writing cover letters, you might consider using a post office box number for anonymity. It lessens the chance of embarrassing yourself should your letter and resume inadvertently fall into the wrong hands. The chances are slim, but it has happened. And although it may not cause any problems, it could prematurely let out news of your job search to your company or industry.

One way of coping with this problem is the third-party approach. The idea works this way. A close friend composes a letter describing your background, but omits any revealing names or places. He mentions that "due to certain circumstances, my associate would prefer not to disclose his identity until serious interest in his candidacy is indicated." Your friend supplies his address, or a box number. Eventually, as each interested company reveals its intentions (and identity), you reveal yours.

In practice you don't even need such a cooperative friend for this method. You pose as your own friend. All you have to do is see yourself as others see you. Or even better, why not see yourself as you would *prefer* others to see you? Be your own third party and scribble a homage to yourself. Use a good third-party name, take out a post office or newspaper box number, and wait for those curious companies to inquire about your true identity.

Actually, you can take a less risky (and more honest) approach. Go ahead and write that third-party letter if you want. But write it for a real third party who will send it on your behalf. You accomplish two things with this approach. You can still emphasize aspects of yourself and the job as you see fit, and you help out your cooperative third party in the bargain. He may still want to edit the letter to reflect his personal style, but you've made it a lot easier for him than if he had to write the entire letter from scratch.

Timing: An Important Part of the Game

Once your letter is finished, you can just send it out, right? Not exactly. Timing is another crucial element here. Most of us have been taught that speed is essential, and as a result, some people believe they must practically camp at the main post office with their newspaper ads and typewriter. On the other hand, some of the "progressive" job-hunt manuals would nudge you into waiting a full two weeks or so before answering an ad. They reason from the following distribution of responses received by a typical company from their Sunday ad:

Sunday— 2 applications. (Friends of these two job seekers worked at the newspaper and copied the job notices the night before. The candidates then spent Saturday night typing the letters and sent them special delivery to get them there on Sunday.)

Monday— 25 applications. (These people got the paper bright and early Sunday and dashed off those letters in time for the 9 A.M. mail pickup.)

Tuesday— 33 applications. (These applicants received the paper at noon Sunday and mailed letters by 11 P.M. that night.)

*Wednesday—*47 applications. (They had picked up the ads even later, read them over Monday morning coffee, and sent letters that afternoon.)

Thursday— 24 applications; *Friday—*13 applications; *Saturday and beyond—*9 applications.

It's true, as some job-hunt advisers reason, that many personnel managers will be sick to death of looking at resumes on Monday, Tuesday, and Wednesday. But you cannot afford to wait forever. Waiting two full weeks may get you the personnel man's strict and undivided attention, but by then there may be no job opening left. You want to get to him sooner than that, and pop in right after the peak of responses. Shooting for Thursday or Friday seems to be the best bet.

The Numbers Game and Its Variations

Along with timing comes the problem of competition in numbers. You want to do something to increase your odds of being noticed. One logical method exploits the very fact that there is a deluge of responses. Simply go with the flow. Instead of imagining your resume trickling in as one drop in a downpour of 600 or so, multiply your chances by sending two or three responses to the same ad.

Remember those people filtering out letters the first time through the pile? Some responses may get eliminated merely because a filterer has had a recent fight with a spouse or a bout with the flu, or suffers from a certain clumsiness of the hands that causes your resume to waft down behind the radiator. You must fight these calamities of chance.

To accomplish this, a few days after you answer the ad the first time, mail out another letter and resume. It shouldn't be any bother because you can just use a copy of the original letter. If it makes you feel more honest, mark it with an official-looking "Copy" at the top. Then if someone actually spots the two letters together, that gives you a way out. (In fact, the company ought to be flattered that you were interested enough to make the extra effort to get noticed.) You might even want to send a third copy a few days after that. It's a way of bettering your chances of catching someone's eye in that crucial filtering process.

A variation of this method is to mail out two (or more) letters that are not identical and are sent to two different people—a kind of one-two punch. The maneuver goes like this. If the company name is mentioned in the ad, get an appropriate business directory and look up the name of an executive way up in the organization whose department, title, or background is related to the position in question. Write a short general letter of introduction declaring your interest in employment with his firm and enclose your resume. Don't mention the ad, the idea being to play it a little cool with this guy. A couple of days later send the usual ad-answering letter to the person mentioned in the ad.

Now, the first letter will often do you no good at all. But occasionally (enough to make it worth a try), Mr. Biggie (the higher-up) will do one of two encouraging things. The first possibility is that he will be thrilled at personally receiving an application for the job (he loves hiring key people himself once in a while) and will establish contact with you directly. This of course would be perfect.

A second, less dramatic, result would be that Mr. Biggie routes the letter down the corporate ladder into the hands of Mr. Little Guy who placed the ad. But don't think you've wasted your time writing that extra letter to Mr. Biggie. If it works right, Little Guy has now seen your name twice. And it certainly doesn't hurt if one of those times involved a "Please take care of this" notation from Biggie to L.G. It just may spur L.G. to act faster.

The Waiting Game

Okay. You've finally sent out a batch of letters, and now comes the waiting. And I mean waiting. The only ones who answer immediately are the agencies. Most companies take a while, from weeks to months. But don't just sit breathlessly waiting by your mailbox or telephone. This is a fickle business and you've got other things to turn to, right? Forget about that company. You really didn't want that job anyway. This was merely an "exploratory" letter. And so on.

(As you can see, at this point I usually downgrade the job and my desire for it. Then if the job falls through, I will have known all along that "I didn't care" or "I knew it would happen," and I can take pride in my keen foresight. If I do get the job, I can be overjoyed because I really wasn't even trying that hard in the first place. The job seeker with the opposite attitude thinks this job is great; he really wants it and needs it. If he doesn't get it, he falls into the pit of despair and begins questioning his abilities as well as his desires and needs. Even if he does get it, he becomes wary of the company itself and starts wondering why they ever took someone so inexperienced, desperate, inept, or whatever.)

Your waiting is complicated by the letters and phone calls indicating interest or rejection that come in just as you are cranking out more letters and making more phone calls yourself. The time delay on both ends can tangle things up enormously.

The situation becomes further muddled when, for instance, one day you receive a letter indicating mild exploratory interest from General Motors, even though you know you have never in your life communicated with them. Don't jump to conclusions. And don't get the idea that your brilliance lights up the sky all the way to Detroit. Just check back into your file of ads. No doubt you'll find one describing a ". . . large multibillion-dollar, Fortune 500 company in the automotive field . . ." and requesting that all resumes be sent to Box X 3000 in care of the newspaper.

Yes, a certain amount of detective work is required in this game. There may be many surprises. To this day I have yet to dig up the ads that several companies claim I answered. Occasionally the detective work has to be swift, especially if you are contacted by phone. Imagine: your phone rings, and you are confronted with the following greeting: "Hello, Mr. Berliner? This is Jackie Brown of Univalve? I've been looking at the resume you sent us? . . ."

Note the punctuation in her statement. First of all, the question marks are not typographical errors. For some reason, most Jackie Browns of the Univalves all over the country speak entirely in questions. It's not clear whether Jackie Brown has just started working and is not too sure of her telephone presence, whether she is working from an immense stack of resumes and is afraid she may have gotten mine confused with someone else's, or whether she just constantly dials wrong numbers.

Also, note the three dots indicating an interminable pause. Univalve is now patiently awaiting my response. But to what? Other than answering "yes," there's not much else to say. I usually take one of two approaches with these callers. If neither "Univalve" nor "Brown" sounds familiar, I just charge right in. "Uh . . . oh, yes . . . Miss Brown, Univalve. I'm quite happy you called. I assume you want to set up an interview."

Let's face it, whether you remember writing to them or not, you've got nothing to lose. She has your resume, so you must have been interested in the job sometime in your life. Also, in your reply you haven't said anything untrue. You have simply stayed even in the race without revealing your position. The baton is passed back to her at this point, and you can talk about setting up the interview.

This is the strategy to take most of the time. However, what if your job objectives have changed over the last couple of months and you don't want to interview with just any company? Then I would simply stall for a moment: "Yes, thank you, Miss Brown. I appreciate your call. But would you excuse me and hold for just a moment?"

What am I doing? I'm merely stalling so I can quickly slip out my letter folder and dig out the ad and the copy of the letter I sent. It would be nice to know the exact ad and job she is talking about so I can decide whether or not to pursue it. And remember that if you don't find the ad in your file, you haven't lost much since you can just get back on the phone and pick up where you left off.

I should mention one problem associated with the telephone call. Sometime during your conversation with the secretary or assistant who placed the call you may want to ask a question or two about the job. Since the boss is the one doing the hiring, the secretary may know very little about the position. He or she doesn't want to spend too much time with you since there are other calls to make and meetings to set up.

Still, I suppose you can't lose much by slipping in one or two pertinent questions to gain more information. Who knows, maybe the boss will get on the phone and help you out. But be careful. Your goal is to be invited for a face-to-face interview. Wouldn't you hate to be eliminated from consideration solely on the basis of your telephone personality?

Along with unexplainable replies or confusing phone calls, you may receive *no* answer at all from many companies. They are just making things easier for themselves. There may have been no job available in the first place, or perhaps they were merely getting a feel for the marketplace. Or, if the ad had been placed in good faith, there may have been a subsequent job freeze and they're not hiring anymore. Perhaps your letter or theirs got lost in the mail.

Actually, these are rationalizations. Let's face it, with the large numbers of people applying to most ads, many are not even going to come close to filling the bill. So an employer must say no to a lot of people. Or, more simply, he'll say nothing at all to the unsuccessful ones. That is the easiest thing to do, and that's why so many companies use blind ads in the first place. They don't have to bother rejecting all those people.

Timing is another problem in answering ads. Because of the variable delays in hearing from companies, it is difficult to decide whether or not you have been rejected. Just because you hear nothing within two weeks from the time you sent out your letter might not mean much. The way some places work, it may have taken that long for your letter to get from the mailroom to the personnel department. To be on the safe side, I give companies a good two months before I write them off as prospects.

After two months, however, you might want to amuse yourself by sending follow-up letters to these silent companies (or box numbers). I say "amuse" because, in all honesty, do you really think such companies will take the time to answer an applicant's follow-up letter? But if you feel uncomfortable writing off every last one of the jobs you applied for, just follow up the really juicy ads, the ones with the fascinating descriptions or good salaries. Casually drop them a line about "that job you advertised a while ago" and give them a quick soft sell with an applicable part of your background. Use your original letter as a base. If you get no answer after that, assume that the ad was placed by some agency out to reap a harvest of resumes.

Good News and Bad News

Some of the responses you'll get are neither encouraging nor discouraging. Finding an employment application form in the return mail is not the most uplifting experience. And not the most informative either. But most of us feel compelled to complete it and send it back. It is unfortunate that many personnel departments require this dull form to be completed before they allow their company's departments to proceed in their search for candidates. It's not only dull, it's time-consuming. But there are ways to turn the tables and make the application form more interesting both for yourself and the company.

The best time-saver is the most obvious. Eliminate drudgery by not writing anything more than once. You've given them items like "Education" and "Work Experience" before, right? Skip all that and write "See Resume" in the appropriate space. Some personnel departments get heartburn over this, but as long as you remember to attach an extra copy of your resume, they usually succumb. Why should they want to wade through that material twice, any more than you do? Besides, a snazzy resume can only liven up a stodgy application form.

The very end of an application form is often the most amusing part. After you have plowed through question after question dealing with every aspect of your waking life, they ask you to "indicate any additional information you think would be helpful for us to know." (In more solemn establishments, it's simply billed as "Miscellaneous Accomplishments.")

This is like playing strip poker in your underwear—there's nothing left to give away. How could there be? You have spent the last 45 minutes describing yourself. But this is such a good opportunity, it would be a pity to pass it up. A juicy item inserted at this point tends to be a real attention-getter, declaring, "If you liked all the other stuff (or even if you didn't), just look at this!"

Now is no time to make anything up. What you might do is to omit something earlier in the form so you can leave yourself with an item for the "miscellaneous" section. A particular accomplishment could easily be passed over in the main body of a long questionnaire, but it will jump off the page if left until later. And this can only help in getting a favorable response.

Letters and telephone calls will be 99.9 percent of any communications you receive. Until several months ago, I would have said 100 percent. But some time ago, I returned home from an interview, and my next-door neighbor told me that a Western Union messenger had tried to deliver a telegram to my home. Good grief, Western Union? In my family, telegrams either mean very good or very bad news. The messenger had not left the telegram at my house, and on calling the Western Union office, I learned that I would have to wait several hours for him to return from his rounds.

Can you imagine how anxious and curious I was? I finally got the message late that night. It was from an out-of-town company merely informing me that its interviewer would be traveling in my area and would like to see me Friday at a specific time and place. Since this was only Monday, they could have used the mail, and would even have saved time and money by phoning me. Their desire to be different created a very jittery person that night.

Facing the Rejection

Now we come to rejection, which has about the same ring to it as pollution. It doesn't have to be that way. Any serious job hunter should quickly become immune to the pain of rejection letters. A friend of mine has accomplished this in the easiest of all ways—he never sees rejection letters at all. It's not that he is accepted for every job he tries for. Rather, he believes in the theory that a company inviting you for an interview will use the telephone instead of writing a commonplace letter. So he just never glances at any letter that comes from a company (other than from those he knows he has to pay bills to). This has worked pretty well (as far as he knows), except that his telephone has not been ringing much lately. But he likes the theory, and he definitely saves a few minutes here and there.

Still, you never know what a company might do. Besides, I like to look at all the letters to see how well each company handles my rejection. The phrasing can be different, but the general outline of rejection letters remains remarkably the same.

Dear Mr. Berliner,

Thank you for responding to our recent advertisement for a management analyst that appeared in *The New York Times* of Sunday, June 3.

It was quite difficult to select one person for the job out of the many qualified people who applied. We were rather impressed with your academic and employment accomplishments, and we are sure you would be able to make a worthwhile contribution to our organization. After a thorough review of your background, however, we have come to the conclusion that your experience is slightly incompatible with our staffing requirements.

This of course should not be taken as a reflection on your excellent record but rather a recognition of the difficult choice we had to make. In fact, with your permission, we would like to keep your resume on file. Should an appropriate vacancy occur in the future, we will be most happy to consider you for it at that time.

We appreciate your interest and wish you much success in obtaining suitable employment in line with your career objectives.

Cordially yours,

That's all there is to it. After job hunting for several months, you may even become a little lazy and read just the second paragraph's negative sentence and skip the rest. But there are some interesting things to note.

For one thing, there's that remark about keeping my resume on file. I'll have to take their word for it. But when they advertise another job that interests me a couple of months later, I feel awkward sending them another resume. Do I really have to apply for this job when they already have my resume on file? When they fail to write or call the second time around, should I assume they have looked at my resume again and have once more ruled me out? And will they be annoyed if I send another resume?

I take nothing for granted. Maybe they are keeping my resume on file. That doesn't mean they will remember to retrieve it or actually look at it when that second job comes around. So I keep issuing resumes. You just can't count on those company files.

Another thing about that letter—there's the subtle rejection that floats through the second paragraph like a butterfly. I'd rather have it right out on the table. Believe me, a couple of those well-hidden rejections have slipped right past me and I've had to re-read the letters to find out if I got the job or not.

These letters never fail to reiterate my excellent background or to remind me that this rejection should not be taken as a reflection on my qualifications. Who's kidding whom? Then they wish you luck and success in finding employment with another company. They would just love to have you find a job in a company within their industry, preferably with one of their biggest competitors.

Can't you just imagine that backroom conversation at Univalve? "Why don't we hold onto these resumes and see if we can unload some of the more way-out ones on Polyvalve? If we could slip one of these losers into a sensitive spot there, that might be a plus for us." Keep this in mind when reading between the lines of a rejection letter.

Still on the subject of rejection letters, I have given up investigating the typewriting style, method of reproduction, and quality of the paper used. I know people who look at the back of the letter before looking at the front, to see if it was individually typed or mass-produced. Others peer through the letter to classify the paper's watermark and weight. They think these characteristics reveal the company's opinion of them. In my view, whether the letter is Xeroxed or typed, or on 16-pound bond paper or onionskin, only reflects on the company itself. The company has an image to maintain, and whatever kind of paper it decides to use, I won't be insulted by it. That's for the company to worry about.

6 / How the Physical Setting Can Unsettle You

EVERY actor knows that scenery and choreography can greatly affect a play's impact. There is an analogous situation in job hunting: the contrived atmosphere of the job interview has a calculated effect on you.

Setting the Stage in the Waiting Room

You have managed to find the right building, floor, and reception area, and you have announced yourself to the receptionist. She answers, "An appointment with Mr. Graham? If you'll just have a seat, I'll see if he is in."

See if he is in? He has to be in. His secretary called only yesterday to set up this appointment! Oh well, keep all this to yourself. The receptionist hasn't the time to listen anyway; she's busy talking to Mr. Graham. "Please have a seat. Mr. Graham will be ready to see you in a moment."

Now don't you wish you had Superman's X-ray vision so you could see right into Graham's office and watch him get ready? There he is fixing his tie, combing his hair, arranging the papers on his desk into neat piles of creativity, and trying to remember where he put your resume. At least, that's what you imagine. After all, he's only human and needs time to collect himself. If it happens to be early afternoon, Graham may also be finishing his lunch and hoping that you, his first interviewee of the afternoon, will not give him indigestion.

While in the waiting room, have a look around. These reception areas can be quite different in size, quality, reading material, lighting, and so on. Company designers usually try to make them impressive, since this often is also where their customers enter. How it is set up can give you clues about the company's self-image.

For example, take a look at the magazines and other reading material scattered around the room. Find *Business Week, Forbes, Fortune,* or *Barron's,* and you know this place is all business. Do they imagine you feel comfortable enough to read this stuff? Anyway, this doesn't sound like a place where you can relax and unwind if all they can read about is business. All work and no play, you know.

How about *The New Yorker, Psychology Today, Harper's,* and *The Atlantic Monthly?* This seems like an obvious attempt to appear intellectual. I don't like the pretense. *Time, Newsweek, U.S. News and World Report?*

A little better, but it always seems that the particular issue on the table features a story on the bad shape of the current business environment or employment picture or Gross National Product. Who needs that?

The local newspaper, plus *The New York Times* and/or *The Wall Street Journal,* shows that the company is up to date, but there's plenty of bad news in those papers too. *Look* used to be the ideal waiting room magazine—easy to read with lots of pictures—but if you spot *Look* in the magazine rack now, this company is not exactly keeping up with the times.

The general layout of the waiting room can also reveal some key things. Some companies try to put you at ease with that plush carpeting and comfortable couch facing a picturesque country scene. The various paintings are by artists with dramatically different styles, selected in an attempt to please all of the people all of the time. The receptionist brings you coffee, tea, or milk plus an assortment of danish pastries and jelly donuts. Ah, why can't all reception areas be like this one?

Or you may encounter the waiting room that attempts to intimidate as it pacifies. Plush carpeting and a luxurious couch will be there, but instead of the scenic view, you find yourself gazing at, for instance, a smaller adjoining room containing rows of plain wooden chairs and desks, glaring overhead lamps, and stacks of papers on each desk. All this is a gentle reminder of the testing ordeal you may have to undergo, or the reams of forms you will be filling out shortly. The message is: "Don't get too comfortable; you're going to see some action soon."

Then there is the insecure company that feels it needs to impress you with its past, present, and future. Its layout language is more blaring. Glossy annual reports, detailed product description booklets, the company newsletter, and executive biographies litter the tables. And what better way to show you how versatile the company is than to showcase all its products in a glass case that looks as though it were created by Walt Disney? Quotes buttressing the company's image, emblazoned in bold red letters on a huge, black background, are further evidence of the company's importance. All these factors have been carefully orchestrated by Personnel in cooperation with the public relations, exhibitions, marketing, and advertising departments.

In contrast to all of this, the small company's waiting room may not even be a room. It might just be an uncomfortable plastic chair next to the secretary's desk. The difficulty of psyching out this situation might be balanced by the fact that the red tape here is not so thick and you may get to see the person in charge more rapidly. On the other hand, small companies often *aspire* to bigness. So, the "language" of the layout may still be a useful clue.

The location of the personnel office is also an important indicator. Haven't you ever wondered why the office is always so conveniently located just those few hops, skips, and jumps from the entrance? You can bet that the company employees don't especially enjoy trekking the half mile to the main building just to transact what business they have with Personnel. Most likely, the original planners decided that job candidates should not have to travel through departments where people are actually working. So the personnel office is not only convenient but it sometimes gets its own, separate entrance. Companies that do place it in an out-of-the-way location either rarely need to hire people or do not hire directly through the personnel department, or perhaps they do not think very highly of the personnel department in the first place.

Center Stage with the Interviewer: Watch the Setting

Now, back to the action. When Graham finally does make his appearance, stay alert. There are many things you should watch out for. First, does Graham come striding out of the entrance directly opposite you, confidence oozing from every pore, then firmly grasp your hand and say, "I'm Frank Graham. You must be our new applicant. How do you do?" Or does he slip over to you so unobtrusively as to barely distract you from a year-old copy of *Banking News?* These postures must be read very differently. For Mr. Overwhelming Confidence, read: "I'm not too sure of what I am doing—I've got to put on this front to impress you." For Mr. Meek, it's: "I know my business; I don't have to impress anyone." Watch out for Mr. Meek.

By the way, it is very possible that Graham will not appear at all at this point. Not that you'll be doomed to perpetual waiting in the aptly named waiting room. Rather, you may be approached by some underling who guides you down corridor after corridor, past entrance, exit, and stair, and delivers you to your adversary. The tour guide might be Graham's secretary or some other convenient assistant who happened to wander past Graham's office. Graham knows you'll be impressed by the class of service you are getting. Also, it gives him more time to straighten out his desk and his office and to prepare himself physically and mentally for the interview. However, don't be a pawn in this chess game; take the offensive and use the situation to your own advantage.

For instance, while you are being led around, note the layout of your possible place of employment. Maybe you can learn how the company treats its employees in general. Office arrangements, carpeting, windows, furniture, lighting—these are some of the physical elements in which a company's style shows through. See if you can pick up casual laughter in the corridors or nervous hacking coughs behind the rows of closed doors. Do you catch earnest and emphatic discussion of company problems or hushed murmurs spreading the latest rumors? Wide open spaces or tall narrow corridors? Invitingly open doors or row after row of prisonlike closed ones?

I have been told that some superorganized companies have your entire route mapped out in detail (and way in advance) so you will see exactly what they want you to see. "We try to steer the candidate right in front of the refreshing water cooler," one personnel executive confessed, "but we usually want to avoid endless rows of file cabinets. And we generally like a few representative employees to be seen loitering informally in the halls, but never more than five or six to a group. Too many clattering typewriters is definitely a no-no, as is a tour that reveals the junior analyst's cardboard-walled cubicle as the standard office around here. We like to include the more luxurious senior execs' offices, even though"—and here he laughed rather nervously—"their scarcity poses a real challenge for our interview-route planners."

Whenever I suspect I'm being led on one of these tours, I like to throw a monkey wrench into the whole affair by "accidentally" losing my guide and turning down the wrong corridor. It is amazing how this can give you an entirely different view of things.

Even when following your guide, pay attention to any relatively untainted information you might pick up.

"It seems like a nice office here," I began on one such occasion.

"Yeah, it's okay," my guide answered. "Make a right turn over here."

Not terribly informative. But I had made the necessary first move. "You seem to know your way around. Have you been here long?"

"Oh, not too long. Well, long enough to get around, I guess."

I had to keep plugging; something was bound to turn up. "How do you like working here, anyway?"

"It's a living, right?"

What does *that* mean? "Uh . . . it sounds as if you resent working here."

"Well, I'll tell you, I wouldn't be here if they didn't pay me. Take the corridor ahead of you, please."

"In other words, you wouldn't think of finding a job with another firm?"

"If it paid more I would."

Some revelation that is. "Do you feel dissatisfied?"

"Sometimes."

"How about now?"

"Nope. You see, I've already had my morning coffee. Make another right, please."

It's possible you will get absolutely nowhere—except to Graham's office. This is the way some of these conversations run—a lot of untainted, and also useless, information. But you've got nothing to lose. Perhaps a useful tidbit will inadvertently spill out.

Now that you're at Graham's office, check it out. First of all, is it really his office or is it a conference room? He might not even have an office—a bad sign since you would be working under one of those frustrated executives with no office. It may be that he feels uncomfortable in his office—not a very healthy sign either. But if it is his office, how private is it? A glass-enclosed cubicle? Walls that don't reach high enough to keep voices out—or in? Does he leave his door open or shut?

An interview room offering privacy may seem like a good thing to look for. However, don't be fooled—the situation may spell trouble. Graham may tell you he wants privacy so that the two of you can chat unhindered and unbothered, but what he really wants to do is grill you unmercifully with no one around to cramp his style. So be prepared. You might even find a subtle way to keep him from closing his office door; if so, all the better. You must stop him from dragging you into the figurative cellar and verbally beating you to a pulp with nary a witness around.

A comfortable interview room may sound more attractive, but again, be on your guard. When relaxed and seated comfortably, you may say, do, think, or telepathize things you didn't quite mean to. So breathe a sigh of relief if Graham's office appears cold and uninviting. Straight-back chairs, hard wooden uncarpeted floors, bright intrusive lighting, drab drapes, a bare metal desk—all these elements allow you to concentrate on the business at hand. Rejoice when you find them. But please, don't relax.

Once in a while, the setting of the interview may not be an office or conference room at all. Graham's schedule might be so cluttered that he suggests meeting for lunch. Eager to take advantage of a free meal, you agree. I have often done that myself. But I have since learned to resist the culinary temptation. A free lunch is nice, especially at a fine restaurant (after all, the company is paying). But along with the free lunch, you'll probably get a severe case of indigestion.

Invariably the scenario goes like this. You meet Graham at the table, go through the amenities, and take your seat. You both order, and more innocent conversation ensues. Graham seems to be loosening up, but just as he begins his first, serious, down-to-business question, the waiter serves the food. You take your first bite, and that's when Graham finishes the first all-important question. Now you have to chew vigorously and also answer questions gingerly. It turned out to be all too nerve-wracking for me. Time after time my interviewer would ask a carefully worded question requiring a long-winded explanation from me. If I was lucky enough not to have food in my mouth at the conclusion of his question, then I still could not eat for the next five minutes or so while I was answering. Lunch and interviews just don't mix well. It is too easy to be forced into eating your words instead of your food.

Shall We Dance? Interview Choreography

But back to the office scene. Once you meet your adversary, what next? Should you seize the initiative and pump the interviewer's hand or wait for him to extend his hand first? Here I would concede the first move to the interviewer. Take your cue from him; extend if he extends.

Of course, if a handshake is called for, you want to offer one that is warm (and not clammy), firm (but not viselike), and vigorous (but not seesaw). If necessary, try working on it at home. You can improve the approach using a mirror. And to properly adjust the feel, you can even practice shaking hands with yourself. Finally, if you just can't get the hang of a good handshake, make sure you walk into the interview holding a package or something. That'll stop him in his tracks.

Once the interview begins, your first problem is your eyes. Where are you supposed to direct them in order to show that you have a keen interest in the interviewer, the job, and the company? Should you look into the interviewer's eyes? At his hands? Your own hands?

This problem shouldn't bother anyone with poor vision; you can just look in the general direction of the interviewer's face. But anyone with reasonably good vision can appreciate the uneasiness, and sometimes the boredom, of staring into someone's eyes for 45 minutes straight. But if you think eye contact is necessary to demonstrate your interest and excitement, I have found that a long stare at the beginning of a conversation will establish your basic interest. It should be held until your adversary relinquishes control and gives up the gaze. From then on, you're the one in control, and an occasional look will reemphasize your enthusiasm.

After the initial stare, however, you want to use your eyes to receive information as well as to broadcast it. Of course you have been looking around the interview room to acclimatize yourself to this person and company. But don't engage in visual dawdle. Be purposeful in your pans of the room. Look for things you can use to advantage in conversation.

There might be a paperweight lying around that

reveals a latent interest or hobby you can share to your advantage, a photograph picturing your interviewer hob-nobbing with someone famous, or a project report cover page that indicates a useful tidbit about the company. Whatever it might be, seize on it and use it to generate interested and interesting conversation. In this way you can accomplish several valuable things: you put yourself at ease, you put the interviewer at ease (very important), you demonstrate your ability to handle yourself conversationally and reaffirm his ability to do the same. Finally, you show that both of you have positively affable personalities.

While on the matter of eye contact, there is a world of body language that can be exploited. For example, how does your interrogator sit while questioning you? Does he wait anxiously, poised almost on the edge of his chair, in anticipation of the gems you are about to utter? This bothers some people but it can be advantageous for you. There is a certain amount of power in knowing that, as a result of something you are about to say, your interviewer will either leap up and lock horns in battle or be stunned into silence by a sudden disappointment. Wouldn't you rather the control was in your own hands than in the interviewer's? This is exactly what you are striving for.

I used to think it preferable to get the super-relaxed interviewer—the one who sits back in his chair, perhaps lights up a cigarette, crosses his legs, and keeps his hands neatly folded in his lap. Only with this fellow, be on guard; remember the calm before the storm. Inside, he is organized. Excess emotion will not get in his way; it will not keep him from tripping you up. On the other hand, a Mr. Nervous Energy, in his haste, will tend to trip up himself. Also, you get many more cues from him than from Mr. Nice 'n Easy.

Between these two extremes, you will find interviewers reacting in many different ways to your answers. For example, if you have been asked an open-ended question requiring a good five- to ten-minute answer, your interviewer might respond with quick affirmative nods. "I am here and I am hearing you," the nods indicate—but don't assume that he necessarily agrees with you. Similar but somewhat more attention-getting are the incisive *uh-huh*'s or punchy *I see*'s that some interviewers like to jab in to show they're still with you.

Perhaps the most puzzling response is the null response—silence. Your interviewer doesn't reveal anything; in fact, you may begin to wonder if he's heard anything at all. But this silence is meant to take advantage of the fact that nobody can stand a very long pause. He is hoping that you will rush in to fill the vacuum he has created and, in so doing, reveal something about yourself that you would never have mentioned under normal conversational circumstances.

To combat the null, the nod, or the uh-huh, you can try the selective silent treatment yourself. When you seem to be coming around to a natural pause, leave it there and let it grow a little. (For that matter, try it at an unexpected moment, just to keep him on his toes.) There are times when silence is definitely golden. Practice letting your own pauses just sort of hang there. If you suspect he's using the extra time to dream up an interrogatory bombshell, leave him with a question before your pause. Besides indicating that you are not talking merely to fill time, a question forces him to respond rather than to dream up some-

thing else to ask you. You can use the time gained to
think about what you're going to say next.

One response akin to the null is the scribble. I'd
like to see a scribbler's notes after an interview. Judging from his quiet and frequent note taking, he is
either putting together a quick biography of me or
composing some sort of double-crostic out of my first
and last names. (At least you don't have the eye-
contact problem with a scribbler.)

I can remember feeling really bothered during
those first few sessions with a scribbler. There I was,
baring my soul, and he looked as though he were
listening in on a course in the history of Western
thought. The only comeback would have been to hit
him with his own weapon, but I didn't have any
paper.

The next time someone started taking notes, I
grabbed my legal pad (which I now will never forget
to bring) and did some note taking of my own. You
should have seen the ruffled look on his face. His
speech seemed to slow down as he measured his
words just a bit more carefully. Obviously he couldn't
say, "You know that this is confidential; note taking is
strictly prohibited," or, "I wish you would pay more
attention to what I am saying instead of taking notes."

The interview continued, with both of us furiously
scribbling away. But the funniest aspect of it all took
me completely by surprise. At the end of the session,
he looked up from his hieroglyphics for a moment to
say, "I am impressed with how closely and attentively
you have been listening, and particularly with the fact
that you wanted to take notes so you could recall key
facts and impressions." And all out of what had basically been a defensive maneuver.

The overall pace established by the interviewer

may have a great effect on whether you feel comfortable or not. His mood will play games with your own demeanor. One interviewer I was closeted with seemed downright bored from the start. He didn't gradually slide into boredom; he was there from the very beginning. This probably happens to everyone once in a while, but it was most disconcerting to hear his mumbled responses to my inquiries about the job. If an interviewer himself isn't enthusiastic about the job, how can he possibly expect the applicant to get excited about it?

The interview that has constant interruptions seems just as bad. People keep popping in for "just a moment," the phone rings incessantly (why isn't his secretary taking care of these calls?), he keeps interrupting himself to take care of more immediate matters, and the interview begins to take on the appearance of a four- or five-ring circus.

You may find this distracting, but don't jump the gun on interpreting the true meaning of this scene. Assuming that the excitement is real and not just a good acting performance for your benefit, you might respect such a person for his involvement, importance, dependability, and coolness in the face of all the action. (If you find yourself cynically scoffing, then see the section on organized chaos in Chapter 8.)

Once the interview is over, you still have to get up and say good-bye. You shake his hand (did he get up too?) and are waiting to be shown out.

One scenario has Graham rising to shake your hand and saying something like, "We both have a lot to think about, don't we? Now you'll want to head back to the main lobby. To get to the elevator, just make a left at the glass door and two rights after that. You can't miss it."

Couldn't he extend the common courtesy of escorting you to the elevator? Well, let's try scenario number two. Graham remains seated, shakes your hand, and calls his secretary on the intercom. "Sally, would you please see our candidate to the elevator?"

No good either? Then how about this one: Graham rises, shakes your hand, and then personally leads you all the way to the bank of elevators. That's it, you say; three cheers for the enemy.

But hold on a minute here. If you think the last scene bodes well for you and the company, take another look. The guy who sees you all the way to the elevator may just be trying to let you down easy. Now that the interview is over, he wants to play the nice guy role. Also, he wants a little change of pace from his tedious job and co-workers. But you don't want that. You want the guy who is so thrilled about the possibility of your working for him that he tells his secretary to whisk you down the hall so he can jot down his positive impressions, call up his boss to tell him about your great background, talent, and personality, and call up Personnel to stop them from sending over any more candidates. And, anyway, he is involved with his own work and wants to get back to some important business.

So none of this pussy-footed bored-guy-takes-you-to-the-elevator nonsense for you. A good sign is the weathered businessman who sends you off as quickly as he can without wasting his time or yours. Beneath this cold shoulder beats a heart of gold.

But there is more to the interview game than just scenery and dance. Next comes the script.

7 / The Interview Game

THE interview game is a real-life exercise requiring knowledge from many fields—applied psychology, sociology, show biz, sales, music, politics, art, history, language, occasionally genealogy, and, once in a while, biology. Knowledge in your own particular field may come in handy too. You must become a master of the put-on, the comeback, the turnover, the one-up, the me-too, the unsaid, and a touch of the putdown.

The ability to think on your feet (or on your seat, actually) is a tremendous advantage in this game, but a quick review of some of the more common situations should be helpful also. To get a good idea of how the interview game is played, we'll unveil some of the rotten tomatoes frequently aimed at the innocent interviewee.

The Interviewer's Bag of Tricks

"What do you see yourself doing in 25 years?" asked my interviewer. I was trapped. How could I tell him I hoped to be retired and lounging on a sailboat somewhere in the Caribbean? Somehow I knew he didn't want to hear this. Yet, he and I probably knew that my still tender age of 26 and my general temperament ruled out my staying with this particular job for a continuous 25 years. But I couldn't tell him that. I had to think fast.

"Well, I hope to work my way up through the systems analysts' ranks and go into management. By the way, how long have you been here?"

Not bad. In neatly throwing the ball back to him, I had succeeded in implying I was enthusiastic, hardworking, ambitious, and a good conversationalist. And this was purely accidental since all I was trying to do was to get myself off the hook. For a relative beginner at the interview game this was a fairly good move. The professional would recognize it instantly as merely part of the regulation bag of tricks—the standard turnover.

One of the first mistakes I made early in my career was to leave one job before getting the next one. This led to embarrassing interview questions like, "How come you left your previous job?" Trapped again. It certainly doesn't look good to say you were fired. If you say you quit, then you're branded an undependable drifter. Personality conflict? Well, it takes two to create a conflict; maybe that means you don't get along with people in general. Pay too low? This company probably doesn't want someone who is so ambitious. So what do you say?

How about this: "At my previous job, I just wasn't challenged enough. So instead of remaining unsatisfied, I decided to look for a more exciting environment." In other words, you were not fired. You are not a drifter, a crumb, or a moneygrubber. You left because you were seeking that almighty challenge.

So far, so good. But the next question naturally is, "I suppose you don't think very much of your last firm." Your interviewer is trying to maneuver you into a vulnerable position, and he is beginning those verbal feints to get you there. Agreeing with him means disaster, for it reveals your foolishness in staying so long with a company you didn't respect, as well as your shortsightedness, your inability to read people, and your total lack of good taste (and interview strategy, I might add) in bad-mouthing the company. After all, your interviewer realizes his own company could be in the same position some day if he hires you.

You might choose to disagree and declare your high regard for your former company. But this shows inconsistency (love 'em but leave 'em?), a characteristic for which you will not be respected and admired. Why not show off your sensitivity by, first of all, refusing to display either a tasteless disrespect or foolish reverence for your former company. Let the interviewer feel a twinge of embarrassment for asking the question. Then give him a brief but differently phrased reiteration of your desire for the important challenge. Say, "Oh, that's not necessarily true." Let that sink in, and then add, "There was simply no real opportunity there." That ought to silence him.

If you are still working and seeking employment, don't expect to escape the last barrage of questions. The interviewer may phrase the question differently, but his intent is the same. After all, asking "Why do you want to leave your present position?" isn't much different from asking "How come you left your previous job?" It's just a little less embarrassing.

In any case, your answer to the notorious question about your reasons for leaving the job can be essentially the same, whether you're still employed or not. The obvious difference lies in your (and your interviewer's) mental state: being in a job tends to give you more self-confidence and makes your story somewhat more convincing.

After some probes about your background, you might hear a question like, "Do you work better on your own or as part of a group?" Now this can become a little tricky. Some jobs are clearly ivory tower positions requiring a self-starter, someone who works well as a loner. Others will obviously require much more personal contact and group problem solving. And, of course, many jobs fall somewhere in between. But the job might not have been all that well defined yet, and your interviewer may be trying to coax you into revealing your preferences before he reveals his. That is not being very cooperative, is it?

Although it's better to have some idea of the job description, a useful, but weaker, defense is to steer a careful middle course. "I work well as part of a group because I generate ideas and keep the group moving. Of course this also makes it easy for me to adapt to working alone since I am generally able to carry out my own ideas." This covers both possibilities but doesn't concede anything to the interviewer.

Another frequent question is, "Have you been having much trouble finding a job?" Once again there is the implication that you are unwanted. After all, if the other companies didn't take you, why should this one?

This calls for a reply laced with a bit of the unsaid: "Actually I have just been trying to be somewhat selective in choosing the next step in my career." Well now, there was more than just a bit of the unsaid there. First, it sounds as though you received at least several job offers that were not up to your expectations. This indicates your desirability. Second, it implies that your next, all-important step will be a permanent one (note the reference to career rather than job). Finally, since you take these decisions so seriously, once you receive an offer from your dream company, presumably you will run to accept it quickly because you know exactly what you're looking for.

Once the interviewer sees you are choosy, his curiosity may be aroused enough for him to ask, "What other companies have you been speaking with?" Pretty nosy, isn't he? Of course he may just be trying to gather more information about you, but most likely he doesn't believe your challenge-and-opportunity story. He is looking for you to hesitate that fraction of a second that will tell him you are lying. Needless to say, don't hesitate! Tell him right away it's none of his business! Well, not exactly like that; it might be better to say, "I would rather not answer because I don't want to abuse the confidentiality of the talks I've had with some of your competitors." That's known as the downshift, a move that takes the listener's focus away from your negative response and over to the latter part of your statement. Can't you just see the word "competitors" jiggling his eyeballs, getting caught in his throat? At the very least, it should knock him a bit off balance.

By the way, it's all right to trip him up, but don't give him vertigo. For example, if he asks about your family background, don't make it hard on him by confessing that your uncle is a convicted ax murderer. Don't embarrass your interviewer with an answer that could give rise to all sorts of nasty associations. The point is to respond with an aura of confidence and good intentions so that even an answer he disagrees with can be easily rationalized or smoothed over in his mind.

Still using a negative line of questioning, your interviewer may ask, "What do you consider your greatest weaknesses?" (The experienced interviewer may more carefully ask, "What areas need further development?") Can they really ask such brazen questions? you might wonder. And do they really expect you to answer them? Well, whether they can or can't is less relevant than the fact that they do, and they do expect an answer.

Since we all have weaknesses, it would be folly to reply, "At the moment I can't think of any." Rather than take you at your word, your interviewer would immediately infer that two definite weaknesses of yours are an overblown ego and a faulty memory. That kind of statement only gets you into deeper water.

So, the question must be confronted head on. But how direct can you be? Should you admit, "I have trouble dealing with people in a business situation" even if this is really the case? Assuming you are applying for one of the majority of jobs that involve dealing with people in a business situation, you would have to be out of your mind to admit that. And insanity certainly is another, more serious weakness that I would take great pains not to reveal.

Instead, you could say, "Sometimes I get impatient with my co-workers to complete a job accurately and expediently." Get the picture? The trick is to declare a trait in such a way that it comes across as a strong point. If you feel that you are a pushy individual, then you can admit that "I tend to drive myself and others a bit too much." An argumentative person could say, "I don't take anything for granted, and I don't accept anything before checking it out for myself." Have you always detested (and avoided) the detailed paperwork often required in a job? That can be translated: "In order to deal with more substantive matters I have occasionally delegated too much of the bureaucratic red tape to my underlings." Remember that in well-phrased "weakness" there is strength.

The Salary Trap and Other Money Matters

Further into the interview there will be a long pause, perhaps a cough and shifting in the chair, and a short, muffled question meant to trap you: "Uh . . . what salary are you looking for?" You've been carefully avoiding that subject, knowing of course that it's more important to be interested in the joys of the job itself. In fact, even your resume has been stripped of all dollar signs. Besides, who wants to deal with this question so early in the game?

Since the important salary question usually comes up later in the in-depth interview sessions also, it will be treated in detail in another chapter. For the moment, a quick overview is sufficient. The pay scale at most places is obviously based on at least two important factors: the nature of the job and the quality of your background (including previous salaries). It helps to be aware of the general salary level for your type of job. Then you modify this figure according to your own relevant employment experience.

But watch out! While a beginner usually quotes a figure too high to his first interviewer (mine had a coughing fit), several months of hunting in the job market can bring that figure down too fast. It is important not to let that happen. A low salary bid can reflect a low opinion of yourself, your interviewer, and the company.

You can avoid this low/high dilemma and a detailed answer to this question by using the salary range—an example of the put-off. "I was looking for something in the $10,000 to $20,000 range." This way you cover all bases. You don't price yourself out of the market, and at the same time you project confidence in yourself. (For more on this subject, see Chapter 9.)

An issue that often follows the salary question is that of overtime work. It's rarely called overtime, but there's no mistaking it. It'll probably come up something like this: "You certainly would not object to occasionally working a little late, or, very rarely, on a Saturday, would you?"

This is presented in such an offhand manner that sometimes a novice does not even catch the question. Often the interviewer leads into it with, "Take a look at this report on a recent project we completed. And by the way . . ." The idea is to catch you off guard. Your brain snaps, "Object? Object to something? I don't object to anything." And you may just as quickly communicate that to your interviewer.

You see, many business positions carry the label "professional." "I am a professional," you proclaim proudly to your loved ones and friends. "I am a professional," you say somewhat standoffishly to your former neighborhood cronies. "I am a professional," you mumble weakly to yourself at 10 P.M. as you finish that project before leaving the office, knowing you won't receive a penny more for your time.

So what do you do? Do you risk saying, "I don't see why I should have to work overtime. Isn't forty hours a week enough?" Not unless you just won the $1,000-a-week-for-life lottery this morning. On the other hand, you wouldn't want to answer this question too enthusiastically lest every overworked executive in the company gets wind of it. ("Call up Charlie at Systems. He's always eager to stay and give someone a hand.")

I cannot say I have licked this problem entirely. The best advice I can give is to agree to some overtime, but do it with lukewarm enthusiasm. It helps to convey the idea that you'll be glad to stay late, but only as long as it is absolutely, positively necessary.

On a related issue, the interviewer may warn you that there could be times when you'll be involved with seemingly unnecessary or unimportant details rather than your usual diet of creative, problem-solving responsibilities. This poses the same dilemma as the overtime issue. Again, a lukewarm "yes" is probably the safest response. This way you imply a willingness to aid the company in any way, but also indicate that you are destined for more responsibility than figuring out the timetable calculations associated with the changing of the water cooler tanks.

A question even more common than the last two is, "How well do you work under pressure?" Obviously you want to answer affirmatively, but it must be convincing. With the previous two questions, a lukewarm "yes" will easily be believed, but that's not the case here. You want to say it with oomph.

You could tell how you performed in some previous high-pressure situation (preferably a job). If you haven't had any pressure situations, well, go ahead and turn a little on. I firmly believe interviewers ask this question not so much to learn about a specific situation, but simply to see how you handle your answer. Obviously anyone applying for a decent job would have to be either quite out of his or her mind or extremely competent in a very specialized field to answer, "Well, I don't know; I've never really been tested." Just feed the interviewer a story that describes a reasonable measure of pressure in a believable manner. That's all he wants to hear.

Be a Boy Scout: Be Prepared

By all means, make sure you go into an interview fully prepared. Know something about the company you are talking with. At a minimum become acquainted with its major products or services, the broad corporate setup, and perhaps even some of the higher-up names and titles. Also, search out some news items on the company's recent activities ("National Landstripping Named in $18 Million Damage Suit"). Besides learning something useful about a company to which you might give part of your life, you gain convenient ammunition to use in conversation. Even if you don't accurately recall absolutely everything you researched, it makes a worthwhile point with your interviewer that you were interested enough in the company to look into its background.

Besides listening to your answers, the interviewer is also looking at you. Let's face it, if answers were all he wanted, he might have saved everybody some time by speaking to you on the phone. One of the reasons he has lured you to his office is to get a good long look at that all-important physical appearance of yours. And here's another area in which it pays to be prepared.

The old "how to take an interview" manuals thought they were clued in on the key appearance factors. From the man's point of view, they called for a neat suit, color-coordinated tie and shirt, shined shoes, immaculate fingernails, clean, combed hair, and so on. But this doesn't get to the real meat of the appearance issue. For instance, a "neat suit" is fine, but you also must make sure it's not too jazzy-looking. A good rule of thumb is to wear clothes that were in style two seasons ago. When you walk in, you want your suit to proclaim: "I'm with it but not flashy, modern but not faddish, conservative but not stuffy." Everything all at once.

Assuming you know how to take care of the rest of your physical makeup, there is one point, often overlooked by those how-to books, that must be stressed. Though you may think you have washed, dressed, combed, folded, and sprayed everything perfectly, it is important to take a last look at yourself in a full-length mirror before you leave for an interview. And this advice is based on experience.

I once was gliding through an interview and feeling quite happy with how things were going; my adversary had been quite friendly, and we seemed to get along very well. After almost 45 minutes, as the interview was apparently coming to a close, he leaned toward me and asked the simple question, "What about your appearance?" It proved to be a nuclear-powered conversation stopper.

I was completely thrown, just shocked by the possibility that something was wrong. I choked, turned several stunning shades of red, and watched my heretofore unshakable grasp on the job begin to slip. Just that small trace of doubt in his voice had finished me. Had I only glanced in the mirror that morning, I would not have been so unsure of myself. You see, I hadn't the slightest idea that he was referring diplomatically to the small beard and moustache I grow from time to time. All he was saying was that I should keep it well-trimmed and be aware of any apprehensions on the part of beard-wary higher executives or clients. And for this I had panicked, stepping on the brakes and going into a tailspin. It might be handy to carry a pocket mirror for a last-minute check. Just don't get caught doing it in the company elevator.

There's More in the Bag of Tricks

Interviewers never seem to run out of questions. One of these, the pipe dream question, forces you to reach for the stars. "If you could start all over and do absolutely anything you wanted, what would you really like to do with your life?" That's a beauty! It has the power to transform glib candidates into models of flustered hesitation. You can't really reveal your innermost yearning to chuck it all for the life of a tennis bum. Besides, why take a chance with such an answer when you know there is no way he could double check it. What you could do is tell him exactly what you think he would like to hear.

Only it's not so simple. Ideally you would feed him the line that, if you had every last one of your "druthers," the path you'd pursue is new-product analysis for a major whiskey distiller (or whatever long-term goals are implied by the job you're being interviewed for). But who is honestly going to fall for that? It merely gouges a gigantic hole in your credibility (unless you can convince him that the job is a family tradition). It also doesn't say much for your creativity and imagination. I don't think it hurts to come up with what appears to be a pipe dream on the surface but has a subtle link with the job under discussion.

You might offer your dream of "running my own yogurt manufacturing business, and enjoying the challenge, excitement, and risk of being solely responsible for the day-to-day financial and marketing decisions." You forge an implicit link with the current job, but still suggest that fantasy aura.

Further along in the interview, you may encounter a question that appears tough at first glance but is really a cinch to answer. Your interrogator leans forward as if to tell you a joke. Perhaps a faint smile materializes on his lips as he poses one of the following questions: "Well, what do you think about the company?" or "Does this job seem like something you'd be interested in?" or "Why did you choose to be a bookkeeper in the first place?"

What he really wants is for you to give him a standing ovation. This guy has the hook out, fishing and wishing for a compliment from you about his company, the job, or his profession. Can't you see the anticipation written all over his face? He's waiting to hear that he has a marvelous company, works in a fascinating profession, is presenting a wonderful job opportunity, and is a tremendously talented and selective individual for doing all these things in the first place. So, give the guy a break. Give him the applause he's looking for, but at least pepper it with some realism.

You could even use a turnover here to divert the conversational flow to an area of your interest. For example: "Your description of American Analytics is very intriguing, and it sounds like a great place to work. Are there any drawbacks I should consider?" Give him his applause, all right, but don't jeopardize your own credibility.

No matter what the interview situation, you will be

sure to encounter the full gamut of questions, from pertinent to irrelevant, humorous to serious, cynical to idealistic, trivial to complex. Unfortunately, it is too easy to get caught in the flow of conversation and answer every question right off the bat. Don't succumb to this; it can make you look foolish. First of all, there is nothing wrong with admitting you do not know something. In fact, some modest humility can be very becoming. It also demonstrates your honesty. (But use good judgment. For example, if asked why you want the job, there is little to gain by confessing you don't know.) In addition, it may not even be possible to answer a really complex question, especially under the abnormal, high-pressure conditions of a job interview.

Suppose you are being interviewed by a VP who mentions that his company has become overgrown and must reorganize by decentralizing the main functional areas but still maintaining enough control at the corporate level. He asks for your suggestions. What should you say? Do you muddle right in and begin making suggestions? Do you lean forward confidently and begin to spout, "Well, first we must maintain the integrity of a central personnel department. We could split up the marketing function, but we would have to increase hiring in that area . . . ," and so on? Well, I know you were smart enough to research the company before the interview, but tackling a big problem like that is not such a smart gamble. For one thing, you'll need much more information than you could be aware of at this moment. But, more importantly, do you expect anyone to believe in your four-minute solution to a problem that company executives have just begun to recognize?

It makes sense, therefore, to beg off from such a

question. Maybe you could suggest a broad course of action you would take to acquire the knowledge needed to respond to it. "That's a tough one. I don't think I could answer that right now. I'd have to explore the problem for a few weeks before I could generate some alternatives. At a minimum, I would want to talk to the manager of each major functional area and a VP in each geographical location." But that's all. No instant solutions. Wait until you're hired, then solve his problems.

Your Turn Now

Now we come to what seems to be a difficult part of the interview for many job seekers. Up until now, the interviewer has been hurling questions at you from every direction. Suddenly he slows down and hands you the microphone. Time for you to move to center stage as he says, "Do you have any questions?"

There's a true showstopper. This one could make or break you. As much as you have tried to exert your control throughout the interview, this is the time when you are invited to take the offensive. So this is your great opportunity. (Don't forget that tactical maneuvers can and should occur before this point. Hopefully you have maintained your position throughout and will now escalate that to a major, coordinated offensive that will win over the enemy once and for all.)

This is a natural place to insert any issues left out by the interviewer. Get answers you need to determine whether you really want to join forces with this company. Most importantly, ask questions that deal with your future place in the organization. Go ahead, turn things around; act like you'll still be the one who is around in 50 years, and ask whether the firm has room for your ambitions. What is the organizational structure on the department or division level? Where would you fit into this? Which branches of the corporate tree are strong enough for you to try? And which are the rickety or rotten ones you should avoid?

Find out about the company's conduct in matters that may have nothing to do with the job you seek, that is, its "extracurricular" affairs. Discuss some of the company's vital statistics—age, assets, sales, earnings, growth patterns, what it has been doing for the past 50 years or so, and companies it has merged with or broken off with. (After you leave, you can check out its references through various bankers, suppliers, customers, brokers, and dealers.) Ask your interviewer if the company has been having any trouble filling the job. And if so, why? Find out if the position is a newly created one. If it isn't, then what happened to the person who filled it before? Determine the visibility of the position, from the inside and the outside, how high up and how far across in the organization.

The goals of these questions are (1) to gain useful information for later decisions, (2) to show your interest in the company and the job, (3) to demonstrate your ability to get to the heart of a situation, and (4) to draw the interviewer into revealing his or the company's weak spots. In short, you can mount a campaign to secure victory plus put the company in the same spot it has just put you. Ah, poetic justice! But don't get too confident about these victories. As you'll see in the next chapter, things may get worse before they get better.

8 / The Interview Game Revisited

THE room is dimly lit, and there are no drapes or carpeting to muffle sound. Your interviewer (there may be more than one) seats himself in a plush easy chair and directs you to the only other unoccupied chair in the room—a wooden skeleton of a bridge chair with wobbly legs. While talking casually, he might offer you a cigarette. You tell him you don't smoke. He nonchalantly lights up anyway and, in no time at all, fogs the unventilated room with smoke. (If you do smoke and he knows this, he might refrain from smoking but "forget" to put the pack away, leaving it temptingly displayed on his bare desk. Or you may be politely offered a smoke and then discover there are no ashtrays in the room.)

Your interviewer has carefully placed the furniture so that he can bathe you in the hot and painfully bright rays of the sun by simply flicking the venetian blind. (Winter is a favored season for interviews because of the low-angle sun.) Questions are shot at you, and the time allowed for your answers becomes successively shorter and shorter. It can be difficult describing the extent of your former job accomplishments in the ten seconds allowed.

Fighting the Interviewer Lineup

The disturbing situation which you are being led through here (or, more accurately, pushed through) is the so-called stress interview. In this you are tested, indeed challenged, to overcome the intense pressure that your prospective employer feels is common in his company. The moment you walk in the door you are deliberately placed in situations that are intended to gnaw at you and force you to lose control. If the pressure gets to you and you let loose one way or another, you will notice the fast pace dropping to an idle. Go ahead, relax and collect yourself. You might as well collect your things, too, because you have just been "stressed" out of a job. Once the hammer blows have rendered you into jelly, the company has no need to continue the test of strength.

But you can fight back in the stress interview. Don't be afraid to calmly open your mouth so you can counteract the stress. Under these unusual conditions, your initiative is expected, even encouraged, and inwardly praised. Show your adversaries that you are in control of yourself and the situation. If the chair is uncomfortable, ask for another. If the sun is in your eyes, pick up your chair and move it to a better position.

The barrage of questions is the most difficult aspect of the stress interview. Refuse to be rushed; finish one question before tackling another. Should you be interrupted, either continue answering your present questions or ask which one you should answer. Don't plod, but answer thoughtfully. Answer only questions that are relevant to why you are there. And don't hesitate to let your warm personality and sense of humor slip through the stress screen. (Say with a pleasant smile, "Oh, that's a good question. I just haven't the foggiest idea how to answer it.") If the interviewer is fighting you on every issue, try going along with him sometimes; yes, try the give and go. Give in begrudgingly— "Well, that's partially true"— and then go right back to your own successes: "But there was more to that situation. We were able to solve a similar problem by . . ." Learn to bend with the stress and make it work for you.

There is a fine difference between the intentionally tricky interviewer described above and the more traditional interrogator who applies the pressure very naturally and without calculation. This is the old-fashioned machine-gun interviewer. As soon as you enter his office, you are bombarded with a barrage of snappy orders and questions. The orders direct your physical movements: "Come in. Here's a chair. Sit over there." And the questions make you more uneasy than you already are. "What makes you think you can handle this job? Your experience seems damned light!"

An interview like this can be terribly illuminating. Question after drilled question, answer after shaky answer, and silence after numb silence. Where else can you get such a clear idea of the rapport that would (or wouldn't) exist between you and your boss, of the sense of his personal style that would permeate everything you do together, the rhythm that would flow between you? Yes, here it is in its raw state—utter slavery!

Other than walking through this storm with your armor tightly secured, there's not much you can do to combat this type of interviewer. But then, why would you want to, if that's the kind of boss you'd have? You might be better off excusing yourself as soon as possible. However, if there is something about this position that you feel is worth pursuing, or if you thrive on high-pressure situations, you certainly had better stand fast and counteract the flame and the fury now to prove yourself. But otherwise, I would scoot out of this one. The guy's personality is altogether too abrasive. Consider yourself lucky to have found out so early in the game.

The type of interviewer you get can change the course of the entire interview. The examples we have described so far are the real thumbscrew situations. But there are other less tense, although just as frustrating, interview scenes. Take the case of the "let me tell you all about the company" person versus the "tell me all about yourself" interrogator. The former tends to do 90 percent of the talking. Either because of egotism, unfamiliarity with the interview process, or beaming pride in the company, he goes into a thorough description of the job, the company organization, advancement possibilities, your future co-workers, boss, boss's boss, boss's friends and anything else he deems interesting. You won't have much chance to talk. You will find yourself becoming adept at the continuous nod, the short grunt, and the occasional "uh-huh." This guy figures he already knows about your background from your resume, so he only needs to keep talking long enough to get a thorough visual impression of you.

On the other hand, the tell-me-all-about-yourself guy delights in asking the kind of open-ended essay questions you see on high school history exams. But instead of "Describe the causes of World War I," it's "Tell me about your education." Surely you can be accommodating enough to provide him with a few tidbits of information about yourself and your background. But don't feed him all the information he is trying to get on this fishing expedition.

Soul-baring monologues have no place in a job interview. So, instead of merely cultivating your "let me tell you all about myself" personality, use an "I'll show you mine if you show me yours" approach. Give him a little taste of your spiel, but then bounce the ball back to him and work hard at getting him to talk and reveal some information. Otherwise you are bound to become a "well you certainly spilled the beans" and "we'll be in touch someday" casualty in this little game.

In general, it's very important for you always to be ready with your own questions. These should be leading questions that you can insert into an interview to help turn the tide in the other direction. In this way, you can do your part to help the interviewer along. Your questions lessen some of the pressure the interviewer feels in continually having to steer the interview this way or that. You merely pop in when there is a lull (or even when there isn't), ask him your particular leading question, and then sit back and listen, content that you have aided the interview flow.

Your questions do even more than that. They also get you off the hook and work to your advantage. With most interviewers, the point is to encourage them to talk. This takes the heat off you and helps avoid some of those heart-stopping, hope-crushing questions that some interviewers like to pose. But it does much more. By getting the interviewer to talk at some length, you may be able to learn why they are hiring for this position and maybe what problems are bothering the company and him.

Pursue these things in follow-up questions and keep listening closely. Then with this knowledge, you can score points later on by describing what you can do for him. Make it clear that his troubles are over; you are the answer to his problems. You can now talk specifically about how your background, experience, creativity, desire, maturity, and so forth, are exactly what he needs, right? Right!

Returning to the various kinds of interviewers, let's look at the personnel interviewer versus the technical interviewer. The main difference is the sorts of questions they ask. The personnel man's questions are concerned more with your personal attributes, your history in relating to people, your general conversational ability, and your overall goals and career objectives, while the technical man deals more with the intricacies of the job you are seeking. Occasionally a personnel man will overstep his bounds and talk about the job itself. But don't worry since it certainly isn't within his field of expertise. Similarly, the technical man, who is a potential co-worker, may be excessively curious about your salary demands or what the company is offering. (Maybe he can use this information when he goes to his boss next week to request a raise.)

Another interview dilemma involves the boss and the boss's boss. This is the situation in which your first interview is with the guy who would be your immediate supervisor on the job. He knows all about the position you applied for and is very concerned about your qualifications and your ability to get along with others (particularly him). For this interview you stress your training and real accomplishments, show him your easygoing personality, and stay away from that success-oriented stuff. Remember, this interviewer is just looking for someone to pitch in and give him a hand. And you can bet your last resume he doesn't want any hotshot shooting for his job.

The interview with the boss's boss (or some other higher-up in the corporate structure) is a different matter. He is not so concerned with your background. Having been around a long time, he realizes that most of the useful knowledge you get is on the job, anyway. He also knows you won't survive very long in his own company jungle if you are easygoing. You know what you've got to do—flaunt that aggressive, career-oriented, success-seeking nature of yours. Show him something he can be proud of! After all, he knows his years with the firm are numbered, and he wants to leave the company in good hands.

Questions, Questions, and More Questions

Some interviewers like to throw in test questions so they can gauge the applicant's technical ability in his particular field. There are three basic types of questions: the password test, the name game, and Beat the Clock.

The password test comes when the interviewer casually reels off a number of key technical terms to see how intelligently you field them. The name game is similar, but instead of tossing around jargon, he selects names you should know of professors at your school and experts or authors in your field and injects them into the conversation to test your awareness.

The last type, Beat the Clock, is potentially the most damaging. Once in a rare while, an interviewer will present a hypothetical (or not so hypothetical) problem in your field for you to solve. There is really no way of preparing for this, other than somehow being generally good at what you do. Anyway, it is fairly infrequent, so it's not worth worrying about; you'll just have to do it. But you should be aware of the sneaky Beat the Clock practitioner who is really only hunting for a solution to a problem and doesn't necessarily need an employee to fill a position. He figures he might attract a few candidates from his industry competitors and then milk them for information. At the very least he will gather some intelligent outsiders who might apply some unbiased insight to the problem. But he still may end up not hiring anyone at all.

In the "Say the secret word and win $500" ploy—closely related to the name game—there isn't much you can do to make it work for you, other than to recognize it is happening. While the interviewer is talking, he may try to sprinkle into the conversation various key names or phrases selected to ring a familiar bell in the interviewee's mind—a bell that declares "He went to the same school I did" or "He is a member of the same national fraternity" or "He is a big member of the same church as me." These mutual associations are what separate "them" from "us."

The cues are not always verbal; there can be some subtle gesture that hints at the potential bond—a handshake, a well-placed wink, a stroll, a shuffle, a smile, a raised eyebrow. The cues can also come from articles of clothing or jewelry. Whatever the vehicle, the message is there—"Are you . . . ? Have you . . . ? Do you . . . ?"—and it screams out for a cognitive response that lets your interviewer know there is something the two of you share and can identify with.

The entire scene can be rather heartwarming if you happen to hit the right secret word or gesture. There are those times, though, when the two of you cannot seem to find that common bond. Unfortunately this interview ploy cannot be anticipated, and your response cannot easily be faked.

Fakery from your opponent's side of the desk occurs frequently enough. People who feel uncomfortable interviewing others must find shelter in some subterfuge so they can relax. First, there is the simple case of inexperience, which can be real or practiced.

True inexperience is exemplified by the fellow who joined the firm's personnel department only a month ago, fresh out of school. There is no way he could be expected to have experience, and there is only one way he's going to get it—on-the-job training in interviewing you and dozens of others.

In contrast to this is practiced or "professional" inexperience, the kind that takes years to develop into a fine art. I fail to be awed by the professional who takes a potentially lively interview and manages to transform it into intellectual deadwood.

A shelter often used by the inexperienced is the verbatim gamut. Glancing over your resume, the interviewer catches an interesting point. "It says here that you spent two years with Mobil Oil," he begins, somehow managing to mix a trace of disbelief with a smidgeon of interest.

It says here? Big surprise—he's reading your resume, not the *World Book Encyclopedia!*

"Hmmm," he continues in the same vein, hoping that you catch on and decide to defend your background as represented by your resume (his security blanket). After you explain the Mobil Oil job, he goes on, "Before that you did some simulation work for the drug subsidiary of an international conglomerate?" Right again, word for word.

He wants you to pick up the ball and run with it. On and on it goes. A statement is lifted verbatim from your resume, a hesitant question mark is added, and you are given the hint to expound on the topic. The best remedy you could hope for is a good stiff breeze that would loft your resume (his crutch) off his desk and into the wild blue yonder. Then he'd really have to improvise!

A close cousin of the verbatim gamut is the punchcard interview. Here questions are asked so mechanically, you are convinced the interviewer is more bored than you are. Well, he should be; he insists on posing the same questions, in the same order and with the same timing, to every candidate he sees. Perhaps he argues that everyone must be judged under completely equal conditions. Good employees exhibit certain distinguishing characteristics. He'll easily spot a wanderer from the norm—and eliminate him in a hurry.

Whom Are You Talking to?

Most people you'll see are primary interviewers, those who have some direct stake in you and the job you applied for. But you may run into the secondary interviewer. He is, say, a guy working in another department entirely, or even for another company, who has volunteered to help out his friend—your prospective boss—by chatting with you for a while. Or it just may be that your would-be boss is trying to collect a few points by letting an associate feel he's lending his judgment.

The secondary interviewer's disinterested position makes him pivotally important to you. He couldn't care less if he impresses you or not. You won't be with him for long. He will slip in a couple of questions amid the usual background chatter. These questions have been hammered out of previous, similar sessions and have withstood the test of time for their shock value and irrelevancy.

Remember those questions you may have come across in the employment literature which you pooh-poohed as nigh unto impossible to encounter in a real interview? Well, if you find yourself with a secondary interviewer, you will swear off pooh-poohing for good. You're going to have some beauties casually tossed your way.

Since you don't encounter the secondary interviewer in most cases until you are well into the second round of interviews, you will often have some warning, so you can prepare for it. For this guy, ease off on trying to emphasize the perfect blend of the job and your background. Instead, load up on the personal factor. Take the attitude that it is not so much that you are right for the job but that you are right, period! And if you don't bag the original job, who knows but that you might salvage something out of this low-key interview.

Actually, being interviewed by more than one person in the company can sometimes be very instructive for you, even amusing. Here you can store a couple of key topics in your mind beforehand, and then ask each interviewer a few questions dealing with those topics. It can be very informative to see how different people in the same company handle the same subject.

The substitute interview, on the other hand, is a fairly useless exercise for all concerned, and this becomes evident very quickly. For some reason (perhaps an eleventh-hour crisis), your scheduled interrogator has been replaced by a surprised and unprepared stand-in who is quietly uninterested in you, or the job or your desire for it. This is a terribly frustrating situation for both of you. But you can salvage something out of this dead end. Use the opportunity to delve into aspects of the general working conditions. Maybe he will offer his third-party thoughts about working with (or against) the department whose niche you are aiming to fill. His once-removed point of view can help you avoid short-sighted mistakes.

Another mostly fruitless situation is the hodge-podge interview. You have set up your interview at least a week in advance and when you arrive, you discover employees of the firm scurrying anxiously about as though the company's sky has fallen. In reality, it has. And your interview takes place within this atmosphere of turmoil. The company's leading division may have sadly announced a precipitous drop in earnings for the quarter. Or maybe there was a mass firing of key personnel to drastically cut costs. Perhaps a government agency announced new regulations that would effectively eliminate half the company's more profitable products. Whatever it was, nobody remembered to cancel your appointment.

Actually, the calamity might even justify accelerating the hiring process, only this particular day is not the best for interviewing candidates. But you have arrived and they don't want to send you away empty-headed.

A day like this will leave you breathless. To give the appearance of a real interview someone will hurriedly usher you into his office and slip in a snatch of conversation between short huddles in the corridor or cryptic telephone calls from other harried employees. After ten minutes of this, with a noticeable sigh of relief, he will palm you off on whoever is immediately available. No one really has the time to interview you seriously, so you get tossed around from one to the other to enable them to deal with the calamitous business of the day.

While you are sure to get nothing out of such an energetic day, some companies have learned to distill a useful by-product out of the hodgepodge situation: the organized chaos. It may appear to resemble the hodgepodge, but if you were allowed to step from your interview room into the next office down the hall, you would be surprised to find a most peaceful scene there. Likewise everywhere else in the corporation. The hurricane of anxious activity revolves about you alone. It is all a plot to see how you can handle the fast pace that often accompanies sudden corporate crises. Your patience and perseverance are crucial and they want to see them in action.

Though you may feel that this sham is unfair, you will probably never know if the crisis is real or not. But what's the difference? The best attitude for you is to assume that it really is a snowjob carefully staged by your Friendly Corporate Players. Play along with them understandingly, but retain your composure and try to exude confidence. If the scene is a rigged affair, you come off as being able to see through their shenanigans, and they will respect you for this. Should the catastrophe be genuine, your demeanor demonstrates your faith in their ability to overcome the nasty problem, whatever it may be. Either way you emerge in a positive light.

On the other extreme from this pell-mell pace is the chat, a verbal smorgasbord that moves from one delicious topic to another after the interviewer looks at the "menu" of your interests in your resume. The conversation rambles, and anything you say may trigger the interviewer's interest in a peripheral subject, forcing you to delve deeply into that portion of your life.

It is a hunt-and-peck session for the interviewer who is attempting to gauge your ability to jump from topic to topic. But don't use this as an excuse to practice form and disregard content. Unfortunately, he is going to listen closely to the information contained in your answers. You might think that a good defense is to set up and commit to memory a good portion of the conversation beforehand. But at best this is a tedious and intricate task. "If I say this, what will he say? And how do I counter that?" A fairly impossible chess game.

A simpler, though less foolproof, defense against the chat is to select a dozen or so key phrases whose impact is highly predictable. Then you can gently insert one of these before pausing for another question, thus luring the adversary right into your trap, making him ask a question that you have anticipated and planned for. It must be specific enough to allow you to predict his reaction and broad enough so that he doesn't suspect you're trying to lead him around by the nose.

Examples of some key phrases are "But I discovered that in-depth market research was not the solution to the problem," "At this point I decided that my career path could be improved by a simple change in direction," or "This wasn't the only time my boss and I disagreed on the proper course of action." Make your interviewer taste the next question even before he is able to spit it out. Why tax yourself writing the entire script when you can get away with just a subtle outline of the production you wish to see performed? This is much more satisfying to the true actor, and it retains a sense of the improvisational throughout.

A more insidious situation is the Freudian interview. It is usually conducted by a guy who recently reread his college psychology text after attending a special three-day cram seminar on "Personnel Interviewing—What Is the Applicant Really Saying?" This amateur psychologist will attempt to dig deeply into your past and interpret everything you say in terms of the most profound meanings possible.

It won't be difficult to spot this type of interviewer. As soon as you are asked to describe your first date, or how much your father influenced your choice of college, or whether your first impressions of people end up correct or disappointing, then you know you are chatting with an up-and-coming Freud fraud. If you answer his questions, you become grist for his mill. (Actually, it is hard to imagine why an interviewer would give any consideration to a candidate who readily submits to answering such personal questions.

How can anyone who enjoys babbling about child-hood frustrations make an effective employee?)

It probably pays to make a strong effort to take charge in this interview situation and "throw" him, not by admitting you never had any real friends until you were 24 years old, but rather by asking a turn-around question that just barely scratches the surface of *his* personality. But don't dig too deeply—just enough to suggest that his Freud act could use a little doctoring up.

Once in a while, a company may have you talk with a trained psychologist or psychiatrist. (In contrast to the above situation, it will most likely be presented as just that.) At first glance, this may appear to be more of a concern than the Freudian interview, but it is actually of no concern at all. The psychologist/psychiatrist may delve a bit into your background, but he won't be overly inquisitive. He wouldn't want to offend you; you might be able to get back at him sometime in the future, and he knows it. If he should happen to broach a topic that you feel is too personal, tell him so (diplomatically, of course). No problem here. And he certainly isn't going to ask questions that relate to the job itself or to your experience or technical background. He probably knows nothing about it and, most likely, couldn't care less. So, in talking with the psychologist/psychiatrist, just relax and enjoy it.

A most demanding situation is the telephone interview. Here all the helpful visual clues and body language are missing. It all boils down to two thin, poorly amplified voices speaking over a long distance.

In conducting a telephone interview, the employer is trying to cut down on the number of face-to-face confrontations he will have to have. Your goal could not be any further from this. You must reveal as little information as you can, while remaining an enticing prospect to your caller. Give him the impression that buried in your responses lies a rich vein of golden talent. Arouse his curiosity with your mysteriousness and so force him to see you in person.

Have you ever found yourself in the bizarre multi-interview situation? There are two different ways this can happen. First is the Inquisition. Here several interviewers face one candidate. It is really an extension of the stress interview, except that here you have a number of judges questioning you at once.

Second is the Joust, a contest in which two or more candidates vie for the attention of a single interviewer. I went through this once and was floored when I understood what was happening. The thought kept going through my mind, "With all the candidates this guy is eventually going to see, and the added confusion of interviewing two persons at the same time, how on earth can he keep any one of us separate in his very crowded brain?" I foolishly took a moment to ponder this, and my rival seized the opportunity to slip in an incisive observation about business. Not to be outmaneuvered, I injected a clever point of my own.

And that's the way it went—the two candidates constantly on the alert, jockeying for position. At one point I fantasized that, on this job hunter's College Bowl, I would fluff some key question and be penalized the usual five points for answering incorrectly.

But going back to my original point—how will the interviewer remember us as individuals? Could it be that he will do no such thing but either accept or reject the two of us as a package deal? That was a particularly annoying possibility since it meant I would have to work with the clod I had been jousting with in the interview. Thankfully, my hypothesis was never verified. The company rejected me.

**Playing the Interview Game
with the Civil Service**

Taking a brief respite now from the corporate merry-go-round, I am sure that anyone who has applied for a job with a municipal or Federal agency knows that the civil service takes you for a diffferent kind of ride. Of course this doesn't exclude it as a learning experience.

First of all, by some quirk of Einsteinian relativity, the time frame associated with obtaining and attending a civil service interview bears little resemblance to our ordinary 24-hour day, seven-day week, and so on. A letter to a civil service agency takes months to be processed and evoke a reply. At the other end of the scale, a phone call to a government agency takes less than two minutes to complete, and the interview itself takes about ten minutes. Let's see how this goes.

"Come in, Mr. Berliner, and have a seat. We're on a tight schedule today." This was the city personnel office. They are always on a tight schedule. At least they always look that way. "We've seen your resume and have forwarded it to several departments that showed interest." So what am I doing here in the personnel office? Well, then he proceeded into a brief verbatim gamut. "I see you graduated from Franklin

High School and then went on to college for four years. . . . And you have had some related experience in budgeting. . . . How did you happen to hear of the job opening?"

This wasn't exactly what you would call your high-pressure interrogation. "A friend of mine who works in the Housing office mentioned there might be some openings," I replied with brutal honesty. He smiled, perhaps content in the knowledge that word of the openings had not as yet leaked out to the general public. Secrecy and patronage were still alive and well.

"Well, I'd better get you along to see the head of the first agency," he said, clocking out at 4.8 minutes. The other interviews, while not quite as fast (since we had a few more things to discuss, like the job itself), went just as smoothly, and each came in under the ten-minute wire. It took each of them that long to determine that I was not blatantly obnoxious. My experience, such as it was, did not play a very important role in determining my eligibility, neither in direct questioning (though I was asked if I had any "prior experience in the civil service") nor in any checkup of my resume's claims. And indeed, why should they worry about my background at all? Why should any one of them care if I succeed in my possible new position or not? It only makes sense for them to ensure that I can be reasonably compatible.

Sensing that first impressions may be unreliable anyway, a civil servant who interviews a candidate probably says to himself, "He seems okay," and just passes him on to the next interviewer. So don't sweat it. Practice being inoffensive for ten minutes at a time. That's all you need.

Oh, yes, and presence too. I don't mean charisma, or savoir-faire, or an awareness of the mystical; rather attendance, as in the literal sense of "I'm here!" Often a civil service interview will require you to show up on another day at a different office as a simple version of an endurance test. I had this experience myself when I was asked to show up a total of four times. To top this off, it seems that somewhere between the second and third engagement, the job disappeared due to a budget cut. And I was still told to come in a fourth time. Persistence may be a virtue, but it doesn't always pay.

An Interview Postscript

Finally, one of the most educational experiences can be an interview for a job you don't want. Here you have an opportunity to seize the upper hand and experiment with things you wouldn't ordinarily do. It allows you to test some new approaches and learn from the experience.

I fell into one of these situations myself. You see, I had applied for a job by answering a rather broadly phrased, blind advertisement. But after a brief phone conversation with someone in the company's personnel department, it was obvious that many things were wrong with the position: the company itself, the salary, the now obvious menial nature of the position, the organizational setup, and—the final blow—Personnel's snooty telephone manner. As a result, I was scheduled for an interview for a position that had not one redeeming feature associated with it, as far as I was concerned. This was a unique opportunity. I was free to say and do whatever I wanted, with nothing to lose. This was going to be a whopper of a learning experience.

"Please have a seat and fill out this application form, sir," the secretary said after I had presented myself. "But only the top half," she continued. "Don't go past the dotted line." And I, in a similarly automatic way, silently accepted the form and sat down in a comfortable chair to fill it out. Not until I was up to the eighth or ninth line did I realize I had completely forgotten my original plan to assert myself and use this as an experiment.

Alas, it was already too late; the only item left was "Salary Expectations" and how could I leave that out? Besides, the first eight other items were so innocuous as to be almost laughable. Below the dotted line was the information I usually balk at supplying. You know the items—detailed work history, educational background, salary history, and so on—all the information you've already given them on your carefully composed resume. But they didn't seem concerned about that stuff today. I would have to await another chance to get angry.

The personnel man, who would usually be the one to ask the more irksome questions, didn't ask any at all. I had hardly sauntered into his office when he zoomed out of his chair, shook my hand warmly, grabbed my arm, and accelerated me right out of his office and toward the elevator bank. "Since I am a little late, I want you to meet the people you would be working with right now. Let me explain about the department and whom you will see."

He was just winding up his narration when we arrived at the department and he introduced me to my first interviewer. We briefly joked about the personnel man's tardiness and sat down as the personnel man left us alone. Time to get down to business. Finally a confrontation, I thought hopefully. Here comes the first question. . . .

"It's really difficult to interview candidates. I still have trouble with it myself. Well, let's see, I want to first give you an idea of what I am involved with and what you would be doing here," he muttered much to my disappointment. After he finished his overly detailed fifteen-minute explanation, I saw my opportunity approaching.

"So tell me," he began as my hopes rose, "just give me some idea of what you have been doing at any of your jobs."

My hopes of confrontation rapidly falling, I went into a scattered explanation of my past employment. There wasn't much opportunity to say or do anything offensive. The best I could do was to skip around nonchronologically, mismatching jobs and companies. But it didn't seem to matter. My interviewer was positively fascinated by everything I said. I began to doubt that he was even listening.

"Well, your background certainly seems mighty appropriate," he said. "But I want to ask you a couple of specific questions before you see the next guy." He furtively glanced at his watch, an indication that his time was close to running out. I figured there was still time for him to ask some loaded questions and I could finally have some fun. "I see you left your last job eight months ago," he began, and my hopes lifted once again in anticipation of the often asked and invariably embarrassing question of why I left my last job. "I guess you felt creatively and professionally blocked, huh? I know the feeling, believe me."

This guy must make a hobby out of stealing thunder. Mine was quickly disappearing. I had to go on the offensive fast before the time ran out. I started: "I suppose you want to know what I have been doing since then? Well, I . . ."

"No, I don't care, that's your business," he interrupted. "I am just here to determine your appropriateness for this position. And so far, I like what I see."

This was unbelievable. I just could not say anything wrong to this fellow. Anything sounding good about me had been anticipated and amplified while anything potentially bad had been cut off at the pass. Before I could respond, he was rising from his seat and motioning me toward the door. "I want you to speak with my boss. He's a great guy and you two ought to get along fine." He seemed quite enthusiastic. If I got along any better with his boss, he'd probably be inviting me home for dinner.

As luck would have it, the interview with the boss went even more smoothly. I happened to mention one of my hobbies and, as a result, we spent the majority of the time discussing what turned out to be a mutual interest. He figured that the other guy had told me all I needed to know about the job anyway. As for myself, I couldn't care less what we talked about; I was bored and made no attempt to hide it.

Ordinarily this attitude would prompt any interviewer to usher me out tactfully but quickly. However, it should be obvious by now that this day was not going to proceed like the usual interview day. Toward the end of his allotted time slot he turned to me and said apologetically, "I'm really sorry I've taken up all the time discussing our hobby." (Note the camaraderie implied in "our.") "You look bored, and I must admit I have been running off at the mouth. Are there any questions I could answer for you?"

Questions, questions. Usually I jump at this chance to indicate my keen interest in the position and the company. "No, not really," I replied, hoping to be challenged on my lack of interest. Instead, and I realized this a little late, he was totally satisfied with my response since (1) this implied that his underling had explained the job completely; (2) he wasn't really in the mood to answer any questions; and (3) his time had run out anyway.

He profusely thanked me for my patience, and I wrapped up the day by dashing back over to Personnel. I hastily mentioned my desire to leave immediately since I had some other things to take care of that day, but as soon as I saw Mr. Personnel's face, I knew that *nothing* was going to work to insult anybody that day. By his concerned look I surmised that he was afraid I might be interviewing with other firms the same day. "Oh, certainly," he stammered, wishing not to step on my toes, "we didn't really mean to hold you up. I can surely get your reactions to the job some other time." And in a final gesture of overwhelming courtesy, in one last attempt to kill me with kindness, he asked softly, "May I call you tomorrow?"

9 / The Post-Interview Blues

WELL, the "easy" part is over. The job-hunting steps over which you could exercise some control—digging up leads and references, dealing with the middlemen, developing a resume, writing letters, interviewing and reinterviewing, testing, last-minute telephoning—are all history now. Decision time for the company has arrived, and about all you feel you can do is wait. However, why just hang around?—there are some occasions when you can and should take action.

To Follow up or Not to Follow up

Some people advise following up by letter absolutely every written, telephoned, or personal contact you've had with a company to keep them aware of your unflagging interest, your extremely appropriate

experience and intelligence, your limitless enthusiasm, and your everlasting persistence. Actually,
the follow-up can smooth over mistakes you may have
made or fill in blank spaces in your background left
after an interview. As in advertising, it's certainly a
good idea to keep your product (you!) constantly in
the buyer's mind.

So, the advice goes, send one short note after the
phone call inviting you for the interview, another
after the interview itself, a third after their letter
thanking you for showing up and talking with them,
and so on. It's not that they will forget about you if
you don't send these letters. ("Frank, I know we interviewed a few candidates last week, but somehow I've
lost the entire bunch of files, and for the life of me I
can't recall any of their names.") It's just thought to be
good business to show you are interested enough to
follow through.

One can go to extremes, of course. A job candidate who snaps off a letter after every single contact is
going just a bit too far. When you do that, you begin
to come across like a love-starved mutt jumping for
attention. For instance:

Dear Mr. Jackson:

It was indeed a pleasure to hear from you again last
night. You have certainly gone out of your way to make
things easier for me. Last night's call, confirming my
interview and giving me instructions on which roads to
take, was most considerate and I appreciated it very
much. The directions seemed quite complete, and I am
sure I will arrive on time for the interview.

I look forward to meeting you next week. Thanks
again.

Sincerely,

Here's another example of follow-up overkill:

Dear Mr. Jackson:

   Thank you for your recent reply to my request for reimbursement for the travel expenses I incurred while visiting your office last month. Your rapid expediting of the payment is greatly appreciated.

Sincerely,

These may seem like extreme examples, but you would be amazed at what people will do when they get into the habit of responding to every contact.

Certainly a strong letter following an interview is a great booster shot for your cause. It not only demonstrates your enthusiasm but also underlines key aspects of your experience and interest that make you the right fit for the slot. Think of it as helping the company sort things out by force-feeding it the facts it needs to make a good decision. Give the decision makers the helping hand they need.

There are times when you just do not hear from your interviewed company before, or even on, the date specified, and you wonder if they are trying to tell you something. Don't jump to conclusions. You still don't know what it is that went wrong and whether the fault lies with you or the company.

If one of my companies runs past its deadline, I make a follow-up telephone call without blinking twice. But, you ask yourself, won't a phone call just bother them and make them biased against you? Not a chance. They should be happy that you thought enough of them to make that extra gesture of personal involvement. Also, the appropriate decision maker, busy and involved as he is, will be grateful for the reminder (and for the fact that he now has one less call to make).

But when you get him on the phone, don't nag him that it's been two weeks since you talked, and don't make him account for his silence. Get right to the point: you would like to know if they have decided to offer you the job. (There's nothing like a little low-key confidence.) The shock of a telephone call may help swing things your way. If not, then you at least get the bad news quicker, and you can confront your foe directly to find out why you were rejected.

You can also use the follow-up call to put the pressure on a little early. Go sic 'em *before* their time is up; you're a busy person, too, and can't wait around. Surprise your corporate friend by tightening the thumbscrews about ten days after your last interview. Ten days is just about the right time—not too long for them to forget you and not so short that you seem desperate. If you feel funny about it, you can always call on the pretense that you wanted to straighten out your expense reimbursement—assuming you have expenses to collect. Even if, by some miracle, you have already received your reimbursement, you can still insist that there is some problem so you can get your foot in the door. Then you can soft-pedal that issue and zero in on the more important question.

By the way, I am constantly amazed that the same job hunters who feel no qualms about charging interview expenses get the jitters when it comes to making the follow-up calls collect. It must be that the whiff of the kill overcomes their logic. Why freeze up at this point, when the company has demonstrated an obvious interest? Anyway, if they want you for the position, $3.25 for a telephone call is not going to dissuade them. And, if they don't want you, then you've saved $3.25, if not your pride.

Occasionally you'll have to muster all your understanding, especially when dealing with a namby-pamby company whose decision maker has extreme trouble making up his mind. Let's say, as suggested, that you call up your contact ten days after your interview (in which he indicated that a decision would be made in the usual two weeks) and he asks you to return for another interview. "We've got it narrowed down to you and a couple of other applicants, and we'd like to continue our little chat from last week."

They really know how to turn the pressure on you! If it is a job you sincerely want, you really wouldn't want to refuse such an earnest, though perhaps unexpected, request. A reply of, "Haven't you seen enough of me?" doesn't sound very enthusiastic. Still, do you really have to drag yourself down there and go through the wringer again? How do you know a reinterview wouldn't set you up as a willing victim for the re-reinterview and other horrors?

Well, you have to let them know that you can turn the pressure on, too. Another interview? Other applicants? If they haven't made their minds up by now, maybe it's not worth dealing with such an indecisive company. At the least, you can prod them a bit. Lay it on the line. "Actually, I am only calling a few days early because I need a decision. Another company I was interested in gave me until today to decide, and since your firm is my prime choice, I wanted to find out what you had decided."

Isn't that reasonable? This just may pry out of him the decision you want to hear. Should it be the one you would rather not hear, well, so be it; but if he insists on a second interview before he'll seriously consider you, then just back-step a bit and reluctantly agree to the additional interview.

Brace Yourself—It's No

At some point (in most cases), a company eventually comes to a decision and lets you in on it too. Let us deal with the no-go decision first—just to get it out of the way. The most common approach is the rejection letter. Let's face it, if you were hiring someone for a new spot, would you want to personally confront every applicant you had to turn down? That could become depressing and time-consuming. Thus, many companies choose the written format.

This letter strongly resembles the interview rejection letter described in Chapter 5. However, references to your interview are used in an attempt to make the job rejection letter ever so slightly warmer than the interview rejection letter. Instead of "We were quite impressed with your academic and employment accomplishments," they'll say "Our conversation on Tuesday made it clear that your academic and employment accomplishments are quite impressive." Instead of "It was rather difficult to select one person out of the many qualified people who applied," you'll read "It was rather difficult to select one person out of the many qualified people we interviewed." And, in the final summation, in place of "We appreciate your interest . . ." they'll write "We appreciate having the opportunity to talk with you. . . ." The two have a rather similar sound, don't they?

Some companies insist that the top 10 or 20 qualified but rejected applicants be told their fate personally over the phone. This is rare, though; you will more likely encounter the telephoned rejection as a result of your having prodded a slow-moving company by telephone. In any case, it requires great courage and resourcefulness on the part of the company's hiring personnel. I admire people who have the guts to call 20 applicants and plunge each one of them into the jaws of defeat. (No doubt they use the same speech for everyone and merely change the names, dates, and facts to fit the case.)

Don't think for a moment that this personal contact allows a last-minute chance for you to argue your case anew. Your caller may seem warm and interested, but beneath those buttery vocal cords lies a stomach of steel tempered by countless attacks. You have more of a chance changing the mind of a typewriter.

You may, however, find out why you were rejected. This is particularly true if you are the one who has made the call and have backed your temporarily unprepared opponent into a wall by demanding to know your fate. While you have him with his guard down, you must force several questions into the conversation before he has a chance to get his secretary to pull Refusal Script C from the file. (He'll say, "Could you hold on for a moment? I want to get your resume so I can refresh my memory." He also wants time to work up his stock rejection speech.) Ask him if any personality conflicts surfaced in your interview. Was there some problem with your background or experience? Was your salary request too high and mighty? Was it too low and embarrassing?

Of course, just because you ask does not mean you'll get an honest answer. Saying "The boss couldn't stand my guts, huh?" doesn't produce the most honest and useful reply. "Was my background too skimpy and erratic for this position?" is another loaded question that doesn't make it easy for him. Remember, your questions must be tactfully phrased to let him respond as honestly as he can.

Sometimes, though, no matter what you do, you may not hear the truth. Some interviewers like to offer the oft-used explanation that a freeze on all new hiring was instituted two days after your interview. This possibility was never mentioned in your interview, and yet, wouldn't you expect some indication of such a company upheaval to have been apparent before it was officially announced? But perhaps the interviewer didn't mention it because he didn't want to bother you with something that was only a rumor before the company had even begun contemplating your case.

Once in a while you may be the victim of the "structural change." I mention it here because it seems as reasonable as the freeze, and it leaves me just as cold. You'll be told that "the structure of our group has changed, and we no longer have an opening."

But, often you will simply be told that you were a fascinating person with an impressive array of credentials, but that, unfortunately, they realized that your experience doesn't exactly fit their requirements. Or you might even be informed that they have selected one of the other candidates whose "experience is better suited to what the job requires." They want you to recognize that, as incredible and complete as your background is, they managed to dig out someone even more incredible than you.

Somehow the company hopes that such an explanation will give a rush of exhilaration to the depressed job hunter. The joy of realizing that you weren't inadequate can be extremely encouraging, and most companies take great pains to remember and apply this—even though you still didn't make the grade. Well, remember that just because someone else was superior, it doesn't mean that you are inferior.

Occasionally you can salvage something out of the "lack of appropriate experience" retort. If you are reasonably convinced that your interviewer was impressed with what you did in past jobs (and how you did it), but is concerned that your experiences didn't relate precisely enough to the job under discussion, you have one last-ditch chance to convince him to change his mind. He may need you (and *you* may need you) to lay out for him the only alternatives he really has. It's as simple as one-two-three. Patiently explain to him the choices he has: (1) he could hire you (obviously your optimum choice), (2) he could hire someone whose experience appears to be better but who hasn't worked the wonders you have, or (3) he could wait for a long time—several months, perhaps a year—before the person with the right combination of accomplishment and experience strolls into his office. Wrap up the presentation by convincing him that "workwise" you're better than choice number two and "timingwise" you're better than choice number three. Assure him that your ability is transferable and your availability is convenient.

If you can't use this scenario, you'll just have to accept the bad news. But should you send a follow-up letter at this point? Should you reiterate gratitude for having been invited to defend one last time your sketchy background, and emphasize your future availability? Are you kidding? Smother that idea right away! There is no reason to go crawling back on your hands and knees. Or to prolong the agony, for that matter. In my mind, a company receiving such a letter can only form a worse impression of you. "Hey, Henry, this character never lets go. Get a load of the way he's trying to butter us up. What a loser!"

So you've gotten a rejection. Before you resign yourself completely to it, I would offer as a final consolation that you may have been taken for a long, tension-filled, and useless ride. I have been told that there are companies that place ads in newspapers, secure the services of recruiting firms, sort out resumes, send out applications, sift through applications, invite screened applicants for interviews, schedule in-depth talks, treat the candidates to a sumptuous breakfast, lunch, and dinner, hold long indoctrination sessions, distribute sheaves of information about company benefits and the like, and then bludgeon all the applicants with a deadly serious rejection letter.

Why did they go through all this trouble in the first place? Was there a high-level policy change resulting in a last-minute reduction or freeze in hiring? Were there really no truly qualified applicants for the position? Did Personnel decide to upgrade the level of the position and therefore require a new and altered hiring drive?

No, it turns out to be none of the above. It is just that some companies have accepted the following propositions as corporate gospel: (1) they must have a personnel department; (2) all hiring must be through Personnel; (3) Personnel must be involved with personnel matters constantly and exclusively.

Now, assuming most companies obviously are not occupied with hiring employees every single hour of each and every day, let us follow the corporate line of reasoning. Proposition 1 mandates the existence of a personnel department within the corporate organization; proposition 2 says what it will do; and proposition 3 implies what it ought *not* do.

Admittedly the hiring process is indispensable to a dynamic organization. In fact, it is the most time-consuming responsibility of the personnel function. But what would happen if the discontinuous hiring process really only occupied Personnel, say, 50 percent of the time? (Of course there are things like wages and benefits to administer, but how many times a year can you juggle the salary charts?) The department must be kept busy. You'd be amazed at how much time can be spent placing ads, securing recruiting firms, sorting resumes, sending out and sifting through applications, inviting, scheduling, wining, dining, and indoctrinating candidates, and composing earnest rejection letters to candidates for positions that will never see the light of day. It seems extreme, but does indicate that Personnel may be keeping itself busy in order to justify its existence.

With your rejection in hand (for whatever reason), you may have lost the battle but not the war. Hopefully you have gained some useful experience and learned some lessons that can be applied in the future.

Brace Yourself—It's Yes

Let's shift gears now. You've just been accepted for a position in the corporate world! It should be a favorable moment for the aspiring job candidate, but often it is not; some people just don't know how to accept a compliment.

It may be made more difficult by the company itself, particularly by sending you a written acceptance. Fortunately this is a rare bird in the employment kingdom. Imagine receiving an impersonally mailed acceptance from a company with whom you have interviewed and whose people you have gotten to know well. Were you so unavailable by phone that they were forced to use the faceless mail system? Is it their usual custom to send out a formal acceptance in black-and-white and then follow it up by a warmly personal telephone call? Or is something more sinister reflected here, perhaps some internal political battle at the company?

Suppose, for instance, a highly placed executive in the firm has taking a liking to you. He wants you to join the team and he exerts all the power he can to win over the people in your prospective department. Only he doesn't exactly "win" them over to your side; he's shoving them over to your side. So the reluctant group gets together and decides to accept you, but in a slightly ungracious way. Voilà, the written acceptance, which lets them issue an invitation with half-open arms.

A telephone call is the most common way of getting a job offer (assuming you weren't so overwhelming that they offered the job in person; even companies need some time to sort things out). The phone call involves a pretty standard formula consisting of the Meander, the Shock, and the Carrot. But if the guy is trying for a Quick Capture, he'll use the Thrust and the Trap. If you resist these moves, he may counter with the Regroup, Retreat, and Retrenchment. Let's listen to a typical conversation demonstrating all of these.

I: Hello?

He: Hello, I'd like to speak with Mr. Berliner, please?

I: This is he.

He: This is George Hunter from the Safari Corporation. I spoke with you last week about that junior management spot?

I: Oh yes, I was hoping to hear from you.

He: (Warmly) Well, I certainly wanted to get back to you as soon as I could. How are you? (The Meander begins.)

I: I'm fine. What's been happening?

He: A lot, as a matter of fact. Remember the labor problem I said was hassling me? (A grandiose Meander)

I: Uh . . . yes, of course.

He: It's been a hell of a ticklish situation for me. The main problem has been to get the antagonists to see things eye to eye. And it has taken up a great deal of my time. But I wanted you to know that we have decided to offer you the job we talked about! (Shock!!)

I: That's . . . that's great. I'm glad things worked out so well.

He: Yes, very well. As extra good news, the VP gave his O.K. to your request for your own secretary. (The Carrot)

I: Good, good.

He: And the VP said he thought it would be great if you could start a week from Monday. (The Thrust for a Quick Capture)

I: I . . . um . . . I'm not sure I could.

He: Why is that? You said you were anxious to start as soon as possible, that immediately wasn't soon enough. We could certainly use you now. (The Trap)

I: I just thought I'd take some time to think it over.
He: Oh, I see. (Pause) It would be a pity if the VP
       changed his mind—you know how moody he is.
       He was counting on you to start soon, you know.
       (The Regroup)
I: Well, I was just hoping for a little time . . .
He: (Chillier and with less understanding now) I can
       understand that. Perhaps a little waiting time
       would be good for both sides. (Retreat) Why don't
       I give you a call in a couple of weeks? You can
       think and we can think, and perhaps we can come
       to a more positive meeting of the minds. (Re-
       trenchment)
I: All right. Thank you very much for calling.
He: My pleasure. Good-bye.
I: Good-bye.

It took me a while to realize that his swift change of
attitude was based on my insistence on time to
decide—a not unreasonable request. But my first
thought after hanging up was that I had blown it.
Actually a fear like this is usually unfounded because of
the many hours of decision-making a company has
already invested in you. Are they going to counteract
days of high-level, executive decision-making pro-
cesses because of a low-key, five-minute telephone
tête-à-tête? Of course not. Besides, if you need time
then you should insist on it. In the long run they will
appreciate you more. Should a sticky corporate problem arise requiring some solid thinking, they might
remember the thoughtful incubation period you went
through. Should there be some future inter-
departmental power struggle requiring company loy-
alty, your name may be on the list of those who can be
counted on.

Of course, we have been assuming all along here that this job is just the thing for you. What happens if, after some soul-searching, you decide it may not be the utopia you thought, and wish to turn it down? Go ahead, only don't be cruel about it. Think about how it felt those times you were on the end of the rejection line. Show some compassion by letting the company down gently. After all, the company has (usually) had several people working on the hiring decision. They deserve some consideration. Be nice.

After you inform them gently of your decision, shift gears and give them a good spiel in order to promote your talents for any other job openings that may arise. You never know what might come up that could be more to your liking.

The Big Question—Salary

Once you have received and accepted an offer, you are often only at the starting gate. Now there are the salary negotiations. Money is still important to most people, and this basic fact has resulted in a waterfall of books and magazine articles explaining the intricacies of salary negotiation. Beautiful as a waterfall can be, the torrent of oversights can crush you. To keep you from getting further drenched, I'll offer just a few simple tips.

The best initial advice I can give is to keep your mouth shut. I'm not being harsh, just realistic. Try not to talk about money until you have the job in your pocket. Knowing that they want you is a superb plus in this game. Oh, they will coax you and wheedle you and tempt you and needle you. They'll ask you how much you're making, how much you've made, and how much you want to make. They will drop hints of astronomical future salaries. Keep cool and parry those thrusts as well as you can until you know they are at least on your side of the playing field.

Despite this advice, you will occasionally be forced to punt without being aware of the actual score. Some situations may box you into a corner and require salary discussion prior to having the job. But you can at least try to delay the game ("I would rather not discuss salary unless I know we're talking about an actual position."); go for the long throw ("I would expect to make at least $40,000 after four or five years here."), or attempt the safe hand-off ("I just have to say that the position sounds great and I am sure you have a reasonable salary in mind. How much would you say?").

Once in a while you will find yourself boxed in. "All I'm asking for," the interviewer coaxes, "is to know what you are currently earning." Time to get out that mental calculator. Add up your salary and the value of all the fringes you can possibly think of—medical insurance, Christmas bonus, pension plans, life insurance, profit sharing, matching fund, company car, recreational facilities, accident insurance, department lunches, you name it. Add them all up and then say that your job is worth about so-and-so dollars. At least you are still feeding him the truth. And, it sure is worth the old college try.

One obvious point is that the salary question intrudes into a very private neighborhood. I have always harbored a secret desire to turn the tables in the salary area. It just seems that if someone can ask me how much I make, don't I have the right to throw the question back at him? Wouldn't that be interesting!

Eventually, his estimate of your dollar value in this job will enter the conversation, and you may be introduced to a clever little structure—the salary-range arrangement. This is how it was thrown at me:

"Here is the range of salaries we use," the personnel man said, pointing to a piece of paper with columns of numbers carefully worked out by an assistant in the wage and benefits department. "Every title has an average or scale salary and a maximum salary associated with it." What about a minimum salary, I wondered. "Minimum is about 20 percent lower than the scale salary," he said. Apparently, in order to keep an applicant from seeing in black-and-white the low end of the range, the minimum salary figure is not even placed on the neatly columned list.

"Most people think there's something wrong in getting a starting salary below scale," he continued, carefully shunning use of the word "average" because of its negative connotation. (Average? I'm not average, the other guy is!) "But actually, it's preferable. If you are hired at below the scale salary, your scheduled raises"—he pointed to the Xeroxed chart—"come quicker. Thus at below scale, you might get a raise after working 11 months while at scale or above, it might take 14."

He doesn't say, of course, that in the meantime you're earning a lower salary. He wants you to infer that the below-scale tortoise will overtake and vanquish the unfortunate at-scale hare. But that may not be so. Let's face it. Being hired at a below-average (sorry, below-scale) salary may imply that the company wasn't really too sure of you to begin with and wanted you to churn extra hard to prove yourself (and of course earn those raises). If you tend to do an "average" amount of work, you will chug along getting the normal raises and still trail the scale starter. Should you perform either exceptionally well, or exceptionally poorly, you probably won't remain long. The latter gets you fired, and if you do well, you'll probably want to switch to a company that will certify your above-average worth with a bigger paycheck in the first place. Either way, it doesn't exactly pay to start below scale.

From Personnel's point of view, the use of this below-scale system is an obvious application of a simple psychological "fact": people want lots of raises very often. Therefore, a company shouldn't give them a healthy raise right from the start. Rather, it should split it up into smaller chunks in order to give more raises more frequently and so make the employees happier. Imagine a scene in the employee's lunch room:

> "Hey, George, did you get that raise you were pulling for?"
> "Oh, not yet. The paperwork from last month's raise is still tied up. But they said it would come through in another week or so."
> "That'll be your seventh raise this year, huh?"
> "Yeah, don't rub it in, I know you're ahead of me. Milligan's just slower than your boss with the paperwork."
> "Well, you've got plenty of time to pull ahead of me. It's only May, you know."

In general, the corporation (especially if it is one of the larger ones) lays out all sorts of rules and constraints for salary administration. Though often complained about by employees, this body of rules can also be used as a handy crutch for the company, with Personnel as the scapegoat. ("My hands are tied; this is all that Personnel will let us pay for this position.") At the same time it is important to remember another obvious corporate constraint: your future salaries (and in fact your future relations in general) are going to be based on that next salary you negotiate. These two concepts can often work against each other—and against you too, if you aren't careful.

So, assuming you have landed the job and have arrived at the negotiation table through the front door, your interviewer or would-be supervisor will certainly want to know what approximate dollar figure you have in mind. Even at this early stage, it is most advantageous to get him to reveal a few of the cards in his hand before you try to trump him. At the very least, it gives you a glimpse of his bidding range. But at the same time you can't show your hand too early in this part of the game. Control yourself. It's not going to make your negotiations go any easier if, in response to his revealing the salary range, your jaw drops to the table.

Actually, the best move of all is to act slightly disappointed. The arched eyebrow, the dejected grin, the glance-away eyes, the puckered lips, the wrinkled brow—any combination of these can be terribly effective. These are usually combined with the standard echo-back, in which you repeat aloud the top figure he mentioned and let it hang there in space with the obvious implication it is not enough.

"Eighteen thousand?" you say, implying, "Is that it? You must be kidding." From this he is to infer, "He's not going to take it. I may have to up my figure." Or, if not a higher figure, he may push certain less evident aspects of the job to convince you.

(He, just as much as you, would like the hiring ordeal over with.) Once you have allowed him to pour the gravy on, you offer a modest turnaround. Let him know that money isn't everything; reassure him that your primary concern is with the kinds of responsibilities, your desire and ability to contribute your utmost, and the opportunity for advancement. Implicitly confirm that he has made a good choice and has not paid too much for the material. Every interviewer likes to know that.

And then scoot yourself out of the office. Once the top figure is out on the table, there is no point in hanging around eyeing it. For one thing, you really should think about the offer in private. But you also want to reserve whatever bargaining tools you might have for later use. There may still be unmentioned fringes that could be thrown in to sweeten the pot still further. Better to think it all out privately first; then, if necessary, come back later to negotiate the extra money or some other sweeteners.

If there still appears to be an abyss separating the two of you, well, it may be time to throw in the towel. Just don't reject the offer in writing. There is something unequivocal about putting it in black and white. Always leave the negotiating door open a crack. If you don't reject it in writing and the situation changes later, you may be able to take back something you said and still get the job. ("Oh, I didn't mean *that*. . . .")

Postscript

One company I dealt with was determined to get the best of two worlds. We had talked at length about the position, which intrigued me, and by the second interview both sides had recognized our mutual interest and had zoomed through the salary discussion with general agreement all around. The major and minor points had all been attended to, and all that remained was the explicit, firm commitment on my part. But I did not want to give this immediately, and, for once listening to my own advice, I requested two weeks for my final decision.

Now I didn't think that was unreasonable. Every company I had ever spoken with expected a serious candidate to request and use a moderate incubation period to think things over. Apparently their interviewer had a different idea. I was not at all prepared for his next statement.

"Well, that's okay. I just hope you understand that if we find another more interested candidate in the meantime (yes, within the two-week decision period, folks!), we'll hire him. So by the time you get back to us, you could be out of a job."

He sure knocked me for a loop. His transparently veiled threat was a problem. Barring the use of a private eye to spy on that guy's office and report back on any glowing faces that exited, there was no way to know how much decision time I really did have. Taking a gamble, I used up four days and, as it turned out, decided against accepting the job. With the pressure off, I debated waiting out the entire two weeks (with a touch of revenge) before rendering my final decision. However, my better side said no to this, and I called him back, not even one full business week after we had last spoken. I had barely uttered my name, when he suddenly whipped the rug out from under me. "Oh, it was good of you to call," he said.

"But someone else has accepted the job and has already begun work." That was quite a knock-out punch. Cut to the quick, I didn't even bother letting him know what I had decided; there was no saving face anymore. It would only have looked like sour grapes.

10 / The First Month on the Job— and off!

"**W**ELL, welcome aboard!"

It was about the eleventh time that afternoon I had been welcomed aboard the corporate vessel. I was being taken around the office by my boss of several hours to meet some of "the others." I had already met a few of them during the interview stage, but now it was time to make the complete sweep, even brushing into some people I would probably never meet again. You never know at the beginning, of course, whom it may be useful to know. Besides, it was probably a fair way of giving me an initial feel for the caliber and personality of the people who worked there. It didn't give me much of a feel for their names, however; I am notoriously bad at remembering them on first hearing.

I spent a good part of the morning in the personnel office with other new employees, listening to the detailed description of company policies. Of course, these things are important, but my mind couldn't really focus on them. After the group lecture, we split up into one-on-one sessions with a Personnel adviser.

Did I have any questions about the benefits package? Was I clear on all the deductions, mandatory and optional, that were to be taken out of my salary every week? Did I know that my personal Personnel adviser was always available for questions, that there was a part-time (every other Thursday) psychiatrist to handle psychological problems, that I had passed my company physical (a five-minute breeze-through)? And how did I want my write-up in the company newspaper to be phrased? ("A New Bright Star Has Lit Up the Skies at U.I." sounded just fine to me.)

Finding Your Way Around the Company

Very early in the initiation rites you will be presented with the employee's bible, to be placed in a handy spot inside your desk and referred to in moments of need. This is the orientation package usually produced jointly by Personnel and Public Relations. (It figures, doesn't it?) As a result, the booklet is an attractively packaged tip-of-the-hat to the company, describing first the humble one-room-shack beginnings of what is now a multimillion dollar, multinational corporate juggernaut. Then it jumps to the present and idyllically describes the working life at the company.

The Good Life at the Company (or some other fairy tale title) describes your potential tenure all the way from "The First Day at the Office" to "Retirement—Happiness Is Not Having to Wake Up to an Alarm Clock Anymore," with nary a negative word spilled along the way. It will teach you about salary scales, grades, ranges, averages, adjustments, deductions, and raises, not to mention promotional opportunities, vacation rules, holidays and sick leave, medical and life insurance, and of course retirement benefits and various social security benefits (whew!).

All the rules will be laid out, at least those that are straightforward and noncontroversial. (For instance, you won't ordinarily be able to find out anything on the company's firing policies. That is, you'll be looking in vain for a chapter titled, "Fired? Here's How the Company Can Make It Easier.")

The only negatives that slip in are camouflaged deftly, simply by plastering them over with some blotchy positives. Thus you might be told that, should you travel abroad and find yourself kidnapped, you will not be required to contribute to the retirement plan during that time and your loved ones will continue to be covered under your medical plan. Furthermore, you will not have to deduct the time lost from either your vacation time or accumulated sick leave. Every corporate cloud has its silver lining.

It's too bad Personnel really cannot help you out in the more crucial areas. What you really want to uncover is the code of "unwritten laws" existing at most companies. Where are the up-and-comers' offices located? What are the most prestigious window exposures? Who gets the newer furniture? Who hangs out with whom, and whom should you avoid? What is really the accepted mode of dress? When, where, and with whom do you, should you and can you eat lunch? Is much importance attached to the order of names appearing on a circulating memo? (Does it indicate some subtle and powerful pecking order? Or is it merely reverse alphabetical order of first names?) How does your boss truly indicate his positive and negative feedback? How much can you really push when it comes to raises and promotions? With which associates can you be completely honest? And with whom must you keep up your guard?

There are just so many complex forces at work, and many of them can explicitly or implicitly affect your corporate stay. You must exercise your interpretative powers to the fullest and ascertain the answers to these and other questions as soon as you can. Your corporate life may depend on it.

Voices from the Past

One week after starting work, my phone rang. On answering, I was quite surprised to discover who the caller was. It was the overly friendly but not very helpful Dotty Sham from Career Associates (one of my less interested, less active, one-hurried-chat-every-six-months agencies). She had somehow gotten wind of my new position. (For days afterwards I kept telling friends that she must have heard of my job through the local corporate grapevine, thereby implying that I was well known enough throughout the industry to be talked about by the infamous middlemen. It wasn't until two weeks later that I discovered Miss Sham had called my home and was briefed by my wife.)

She was "very interested" in the specifics—how had I gotten the job, who were my contacts, what did the work entail, what kind of salary did I coax out of them, how did I like it there (after one week!), who was my boss, who was his boss, what was the organizational structure like, where would I be living, when was I moving, and did I like the area. She asked more questions than my mother did!

Having a new job seems to put one in a hallowed light (at least as opposed to the gray shadows of unemployment). I say this because no sooner had I answered or parried these questions than I was made privy to a secret no unemployed job hunter ever discovers. I was actually told in detail what types of jobs this agency handles and which companies it represents—no general descriptions hastily mumbled, but a clear, concise description of each kind of job the agency was handling. Now, with regard to the list of companies they worked with . . . it had one glaring hole in it. Guess whose company would just happen to fill that missing spot?

Anyway, we had a pleasant enough conversation. Miss Sham kept throwing questions at me and plying me with facts about her agency's sacred work. I was beginning to see the light. It was obvious that I had left behind the lowly status of the jobless and had leaped into the lofty and respected world of the *contact*. I was now a contact. And Miss Sham knew that very well. Before, I had been prodded, cajoled, embarrassed, bothered, and bewildered; now I was to be prodded, chatted with, conferred with, petitioned for advice, wined, dined, and mined.

I was coaxed to "please let me know immediately if you hear of any job openings because I'd love to assist your new company in any way I can." In closing the conversation, she subtly convinced me of my new important status. "And keep in touch," she reminded me. "If you ever feel like you need a change, don't hesitate to call me."

Other worms began to crawl out of the woodwork. People I imagined had gone the way of the brontosaurus were showing up again. It was as if the seasons had changed and all the flora and fauna that lay dormant through the cold winter were awakening to welcome the dawn of spring.

In the mail one day I received a friendly congratulatory letter from a company I had unsuccessfully interviewed with several months before. This certainly was a surprise, and again I was impressed by the fact that the news of my new position had gotten around the industry. (However, once again the explanation was simple. That company uses the services of one of the middlemen I chatted with.)

In any case, the letter itself was a real charmer (my comments appear parenthetically).

> Dear Don:
>
> We were quite excited to discover that you decided to take a position with American Amalgamated. As you must know, American's growth in the industry over the last few years has been no less than spectacular. And all the indications point to sustained growth for many years to come. (That's nice—they admire my choice. But why should they praise another company?)
>
> Your new position sounds fascinating and lively. Of course we regret that a match between your background and our needs could not be made. (Of course!) This was no reflection at all on your qualifications; in fact, we were extremely impressed with your credentials. It appears that the time just wasn't right. (How sensible of them.)
>
> If there is anything we can do to help speed up the process of making yourself known at American, please

don't hesitate to give us a call. (Isn't that a nice gesture?) As you may know, American is one of our oldest and best customers; they have been purchasing most of their raw-materials, handling and processing equipment from us for years, and we feel we have succeeded in keeping pace both with their changing needs and the developing technology. Thus, we have made many contacts there over the years, and we would certainly not hesitate if you would want us to help you out in your new job. (It is becoming clearer now. I guess they feel one nice back pat deserves another.)

Again, congratulations on your new position with American. We are certain you will serve them well.

Sincerely,

R. W. Handy

Vice President,
Manufacturing Operations

It seems that R.U.H. was just doing a little preventative maintenance, that's all. He was greasing the skids to insure that I'll be all tuned up and ready to help *him* out in the future.

However, the next "old buddy" you may hear from could very likely be an old buddy. At least that's how he may introduce himself. He could be a cohort from your previous place of employment, an old college friend, or perhaps a semidistant relative of your spouse who got wind of your job shift and felt the need to congratulate you. These calls can be sharp memory joggers and sometimes even nice ego boosters. But talk about skid greasers! The underlying motive behind these casual contacts may be obvious to you, but I initially accepted these calls very innocently. Why shouldn't people want to congratulate me on the clever job change I had engineered?

Why indeed? Mainly because these old buddies are themselves on the lookout for a new job via an instant contact like myself. Well, I suppose it can't be avoided; and besides, you might at least give them a break and hear them out. It wasn't long ago that you were in the same spot yourself.

Now you're all set. Oriented and familiarized. Ready to take on your first challenges and begin your first onslaughts to victory. There's only one thing wrong.

You don't like it here anymore.

After all you've gone through you discover that something just doesn't fit . . . and it seems to be you! What can you do about it? You've already told all your friends, relatives, and professional associates about your move. You've invested all that time and effort, and yet you're still unhappy. What is there to do?

Unpleasant as it may be, this really can happen. You learn just so much going on interviews. The complete picture doesn't emerge in the job-hunting stages; it only appears once you're on the scene. And then, if you are really sure it's not for you, there is only one thing to do. Get out while the getting is good.

It's time to hit the pavement—back to the streets again. You've traveled this road before. All the time and effort you invested in the job-hunting game will not be for naught. The experience will serve you well. You know what to expect. Take a deep breath, dust off your resume, and start all over again.

** ** ** ** **

"What do you see yourself doing for the next twenty-five years?"

"Lord only knows," I mutter to myself. "I certainly hope I don't spend it looking for a job."

Index